THE LEADER I'LL BE

BEST PRACTICES FOR SCHOOL COUNSELORS AND DISTRICT LEADERS

I0806842

DR. SYLVIA LOPEZ AND DR. TRACEY BROWN

Duplication and Copyright

NATIONAL CENTER for YOUTH ISSUES
P.O. Box 22185
Chattanooga, TN 37422-2185
423.899.5714 • 866.318.6294
fax: 423.899.4547 • www.ncyi.org

ISBN: 9781965066119

Written by: Dr. Sylvia Lopez and Dr. Tracey Brown
Published by National Center for Youth Issues
Printed in the U.S.A. • December 2025

Third party links are accurate at the time of publication, but may change over time. To find the latest version of the ASCA® worksheets visit https://www.schoolcounselor.org/Recognition/RAMP/Templates.

CONTENTS

See page 111 for information about Downloadable Resources and Templates.

INTRODUCTION

We know the incredible dedication and profound impact school counselors have every single day. We also know the immense weight of the challenges you navigate. That's why we wrote *The Leader I'll Be: Best Practices for School Counselors and District Leaders*.

As two former school counselors and counselor leaders, we've walked in your shoes. We've faced the complexities, celebrated the triumphs, and learned invaluable lessons along the way. We poured those experiences and the most effective best practices we discovered into this book, specifically for *you*.

The Leader I'll Be isn't just theory; it's a practical toolkit filled with simple, actionable strategies designed to empower you on your unique leadership journey. Move beyond just managing the day-to-day and start shaping the environment, influencing outcomes, and truly becoming the leader you envision for your students.

Inside, you'll uncover valuable insights and tools to navigate your path with confidence and clarity. Consider this book your experienced guide as you strive for excellence, amplifying your positive influence on students, staff, and the entire school community. Let's embark on this journey together.

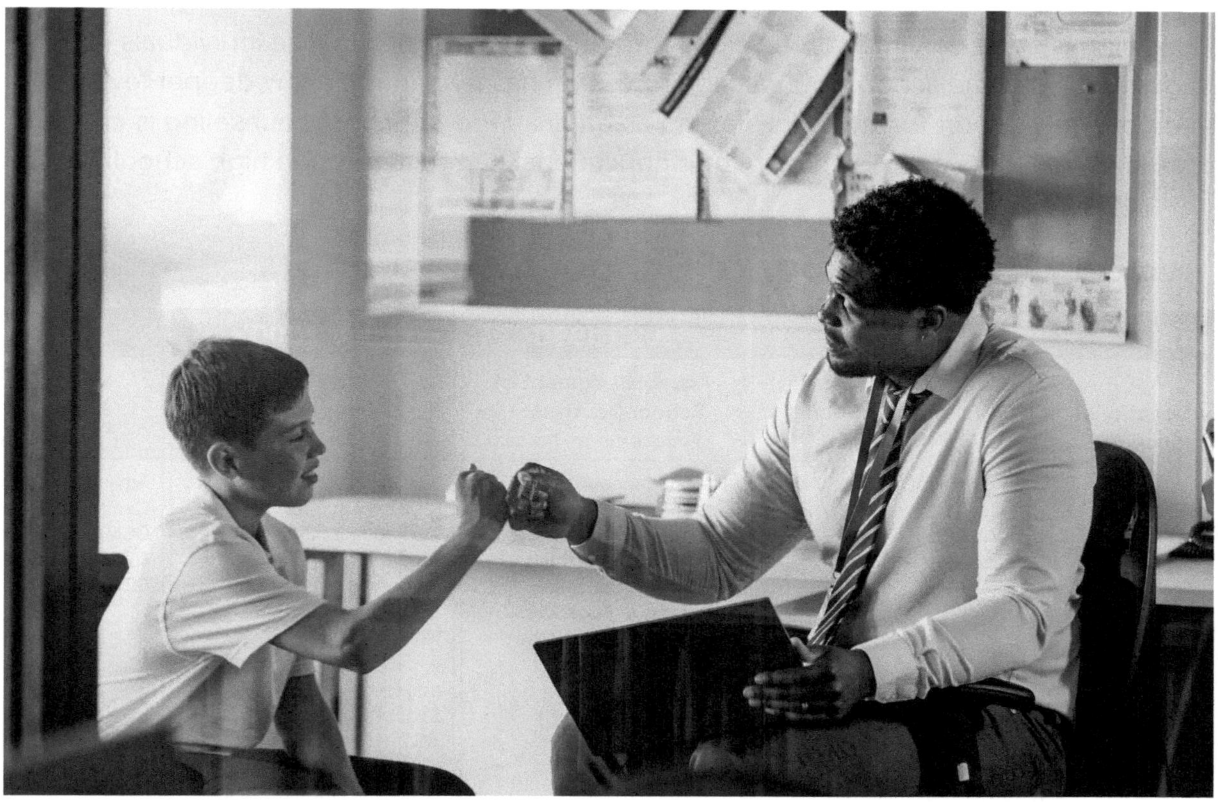

CHAPTER 1

WALK THE WALK: LEADING TOWARD EXCELLENCE

True leaders understand that leadership is not about them but about those they serve. It is not about exalting themselves but about lifting others up.

Sheri L. Dew

Take the Lead

WHY SCHOOL COUNSELING?

School counseling is still a very new profession, born out of the need to advise individuals in need of vocational guidance. Yet the school counseling profession has evolved to allow deeper levels of personal and social-emotional support for students starting as early as Pre-K. School counseling is an important safety net as students grow and develop in their educational journeys through high school and beyond.

History of School Counseling

Early 1900's	1930-70's	1980-1990	Early 2000's	Currently
Need for Vocational Guidance	**Need for Guidance Services & Pupil Personnel**	**Acknowledgment of School Counseling Programs in Texas**	**Defined Comprehensive Programs**	**Postsecondary & Mental Health Emphasis**
Educational, economic, and social challenges influenced the development of our field (the industrial revolution) 1920 Vocational Guidance was a reform movement to change education.	Assessment, information (Occupational/Academic), Counseling, Career Placement & Follow Up 1946 First time money was available for guidance in the schools 1952 ASCA® established 1958 National Defense Educational Act 1960 Major emphasis on elementary counseling	The Guidance Advisory Committee reached consensus about the definition of and the goals for school counseling programs in Texas public schools. This led to the first Texas Model.	No Child Left Behind (2001) & Chapter 33 TEC outlines duties of a school counselor and comprehensive School Counseling Program (stopped offering vocational/CTE/academic counselor certifications) School Counseling, ASCA® National Model (2003) Program Concept: Academic, Mental Health, and Career Development	Advise Texas (2010) GO Centers & HB 5 (2015) CCMR (2019) Mental Health & School Safety (HB 1B & SB11)

WHY SCHOOL COUNSELOR LEADERSHIP?

The job of a counselor is one of the most important roles in a school. School counselors are not separate from the school; they are an integral factor in student success. The school counselors' skills and knowledge weave into many parts of the school. They have specialized training to help students develop their college-career readiness and meet their social-emotional needs. School counselors are trained to help students overcome barriers that hinder learning and provide counseling and support for students who suffer from emotional challenges. School counselors are most effective when they design a balanced, comprehensive school counseling program that is data-driven and focused on student success.

Sometimes, a school counselor may be the only one on a campus, which can be very lonely. School counselors must know their purpose and take the lead in designing and implementing a comprehensive school counseling program. It may start with teaching administrators and staff about the school counseling program and how it is designed to meet the needs of students. Counselor leaders must know how to take a seat at the "big table" with other campus leaders to advocate for students. For example, administrators often have ideas about changes they want to make to the master schedule prior to the start of school, but do not always consider how the change will impact students. A school counselor who takes the lead will advocate for students by helping administrators consider decisions that minimize confusion and bring clarity to campus goals.

Another example is when school counselors meet with campus administrators to review and analyze student data. This data analysis is a great way to help improve student outcomes. School counselors show leadership by demonstrating a willingness to be team players and developing systems that promote student achievement. Along with campus administrators, school counselors can take the lead by building goals that focus on academic achievement, attendance, and student behavior into their school counseling programs.

Leadership can also mean discomfort, dissatisfaction, and disruption. As a counselor leader for many years, I have always said that the mark of a true leader is feeling like you're wearing a target around your neck while being ready for the arrows that fly from all directions. If you are to be a true leader, you must learn to live outside of your comfort zone and use dissatisfaction as a tool of opportunity to help you grow and learn from your experiences. School counselor leaders must learn to push through and move to higher ground. Believe it or not, this is how we learn and grow through this process. Leadership is not taught in your counseling courses. Rather, it's more like on-the-job training. Great counselors do not resist their leadership roles but instead focus on their greater missions and belief that their sole purpose is to serve all students. Leaders do not need a title to lead. A true leader has purpose and passion and seeks to grow as an individual and learn from good and failed experiences.

School counselor leadership requires *courage*, *commitment*, and *character*. These leadership qualities give you the wisdom to know what to do and what not to do in times of uncertainty. No one is born with a special DNA leadership strand. Instead, it is a mindset and an attitude for growth with a "never give up" attitude. Angela Duckworth, author of *Grit: The Power of Passion and Perseverance*, believes that the combination of passion and perseverance creates grit. One of the book's major points is that grit is not about being the smartest or the best one in the group, but about putting in effort and not giving up. It's about failing, learning, and striving for your passion with purpose.[1] Purpose contributes to our motivation in our work as school counselors.

The call for school counselors to take the lead is more than a profession; it's a calling. In *Grit*, Duckworth recounts a parable about some bricklayers, all of whom had the same occupation, but viewed their work differently:

> Three bricklayers are asked: "What are you doing?"
> The first says, "I am laying bricks."
> The second says, "I am building a church."
> The third says, "I am building the house of God."[2]

The first bricklayer has a job. The second has a career. The third has a calling. How do you see yourself as a school counselor? Is it a job, a career, or a calling?

> **A job**: I work from 8:00 a.m. to 4:00 p.m. I'm out of here.
>
> **A career**: I have my master's in counseling. I am a school counselor.
>
> **A calling**: I am here to heal, teach, connect, and encourage others to be their best. I am committed to my students, and I will never give up on any of them.

Characteristics of a Leader

Leaders come in different shapes, heights, sizes, etc., but great leaders all have some of the same characteristics that impacted my own educational journey. When I was a school counselor, I attended a training where the presenter asked, "If you can think of an outstanding leader, who do you think about and why?" That question immediately took me to my former principal, whom I viewed as an outstanding leader. He made me feel that my ideas were worthy. He respected me as his school counselor. He allowed me to be a school counselor. And he always had my back. He was a great listener, always compassionate, always desiring success for his students and his staff. It was my best experience ever to work for a leader like him. As I journeyed through my career, I knew that I wanted to be this type of leader, just like him: a leader who uses challenges as opportunities rather than problems.

These are the lessons I've learned from the leaders who have directly and indirectly impacted me through my educational journey:

A Leader...

- has integrity;
- listens with an open mind;
- uses words for comfort and not for blame;
- is quick to apologize when wrong;
- speaks words of encouragement and understanding;
- believes that failure is a learning experience, not a death sentence;
- has a sense of humor;
- is passionate about the work and the people they represent;
- seeks advice from others;
- has a positive attitude;
- is a team player;
- uses words like "us" or "we" instead of "I" or "me;"
- reaches out to serve others;
- is humble and kind;
- and moves with quiet, shameless persistence.

I encourage you to cultivate these qualities as you prepare to take the lead as a school counselor.

CHARACTERISTICS OF A LEADER

Think of an outstanding leader who has impacted your professional journey. What characteristics do they possess that are important to you? How do they handle difficult situations? Answer the question below by adding to each box characteristics you believe make a great leader.

Person: ____

What characteristics does this leader possess?

PERSONAL REFLECTION ON LEADERSHIP

What does leadership mean to you?

What are the top three characteristics you have that make you a good leader?

1.

2.

3.

On a scale of 1–10, how effective do you think you are as a leader?

(NOT EFFECTIVE) (EXTREMELY EFFECTIVE)

1 2 3 4 5 6 7 8 9 10

SCHOOL COUNSELOR AS A LEADER

It's never too late to start, and starting takes movement and action. The attitude of a leader reminds me of the story of the bumblebee as told by Mary Kay Ash, founder of Mary Kay Cosmetics: *"Aerodynamically, the bumblebee shouldn't be able to fly, but the bumblebee doesn't know that, so it goes on flying anyway. A bumblebee cannot fly because its wings are too weak and its body too heavy. Fortunately, the bumblebee does not know that and goes right on flying!"* The bumblebee became Ash's symbol in the company for women who did not believe they could do it but pushed through the impossible. These ladies learned to fly when it seemed unimaginable. The bumblebee was her company's mascot.[3]

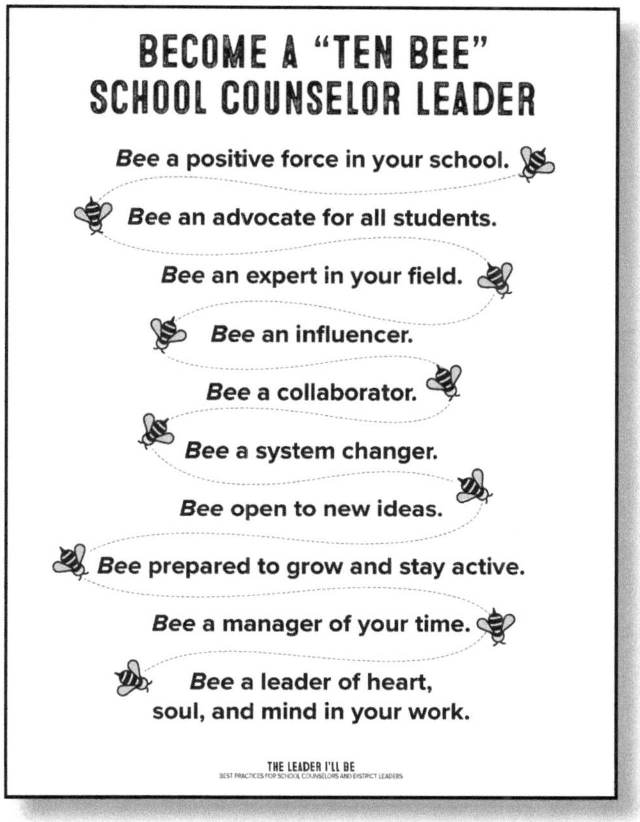

In order to be a "Ten Bee" school counselor leader, you must take deliberate action steps. For example, if your action step is to *Bee* a collaborator, your three action steps might be:

1. I will work collaboratively with other departments.
2. I will help with team planning.
3. I will stay actively engaged in the conversation about student success.

The idea of becoming a viable and trustworthy "Ten Bee" leader reminds me of Congressman John Lewis, who, in remarks made at the Library of Congress in 2020, said, *"Rosa Parks inspired us to get in trouble. And I've been getting in trouble ever since. She inspired us to find a way, to get in the way, to get in what I call good trouble, necessary trouble."*[4] We must learn how to get in good trouble, necessary trouble for our students. It is all about the kids! A reflection page with the action steps you may want to take to become a "Ten Bee" School Counselor Leader is included on the next page.

MY "TEN BEE" COUNSELOR LEADERSHIP LIST

My Leadership List	List Three Action Steps On How You Can Move Forward
Bee a positive force in your school.	1. 2. 3.
Bee an advocate.	1. 2. 3.
Bee an expert in your field.	1. 2. 3.
Bee an influencer.	1. 2. 3.
Bee a collaborator.	1. 2. 3.
Bee a system changer.	1. 2. 3.
Bee open to new ideas.	1. 2. 3.
Bee prepared to grow and stay active.	1. 2. 3.
Bee a manager of your time.	1. 2. 3.
Bee a leader of heart, soul, and mind in your work.	1. 2. 3.

LEADERSHIP CHARACTERISTICS ACTIVITY

Write your own leadership characteristics. Find a word that begins with each specific letter.

L	
E	
A	
D	
E	
R	
S	
H	
I	
P	

YOU are a leader! Believe it!

Take a Leap of Faith

Your confidence and belief have everything to do with the success of your school counseling program. One of my favorite sayings, (author unknown) goes like this: "*If you believe you can do a thing, or you believe you cannot, in either case, you are probably right.*"

True leadership demands venturing beyond familiar territory and strategically challenging the status quo. Instead of a reactive stance ("wait and see"), impactful school counselor leaders take the initiative in shaping success. This proactive mindset fuels the determination to act boldly for your students. By cultivating courage and confidence, you can forge a leading counseling program within your school and become the influential, unstoppable school counselor you are meant to be.

Take a leap of faith and just do it! But this is easier said than done. It is scary to take that first step when you may be the only school counselor on campus. But if you do not take the first step, who will? Learn to build up your courage and confidence. How? By making a plan, taking one step at a time, thinking of students first, learning from your mistakes, figuring out what needs to be done differently, and moving on. Don't sweat the small stuff.

Author Brian Tracy paraphrases Joseph Campbell, the late scholar of mythology: *"Many people feel that they have lived their whole lives doing things that other people wanted them to do because they never had the courage to do just what they wanted."*[5] Don't waste your time doing little or nothing for your students because you have been pulled to do non-counseling duties. Instead, ask questions like, "Why are you being pulled to do non-counseling duties?" "Have you shared your counseling plan with your campus administrator, so they know which students are on your priority list for that day?" and "Is your administrator aware of the impact their request will have on your ability to provide counseling services to your students?" Take a leap of faith. You are in control of your schedule. Your courage and confidence to speak out will serve your students well. Be unstoppable.

OVERCOMING YOUR FEAR OF FAILURE

As babies, we are born with no fears. Yet, as the baby starts growing and learning, the baby will hear words such as "No" or "You are going to get a spanking if you..." The baby starts to learn a sense of failure or rejection. Soon the child learns to say, "I can't," "I'm afraid," or "My parents will not like me if..." The root cause of most of our anxiety and self-criticism as adults may be what we learned from our own childhoods. Fear can have control over our thoughts and feelings. People are not born with a spirit of fear and a lack of courage. We have the power to overcome fear by changing our thoughts. **To overcome fear, you must do the things that you fear the most until you become comfortable with that specific fear.** For example, if you are afraid of presenting to your staff, then present to them every chance you get until it gets easier to do so. Your self-doubting thoughts will tell you that you can't do it, but you have the power to control those thoughts and put the negative thoughts aside.

Fear may hold you back from doing the activities that you want to do at your school. School counselors have expressed to me that they were afraid to talk to their administrators, or advocate for their school counseling programs, or present to a group of colleagues. So instead, they chose to give in to their negative thoughts and do nothing. To have a successful school counseling program, we must learn to keep a distance from fear and doubt. How do we do that?

The first step to overcoming fear is, as author and speaker Joyce Meyer says, *"Do it afraid!"*[6] Learn to control those loud, negative thoughts in your head. Once you do, you will realize that it wasn't as bad as you feared. Your self-doubt will talk you out of trying new things or advocating for your students. Fear keeps you in your comfort zone, which limits your ability to do exciting and creative things. Be willing and open to recognize that there is a silver lining for every fear of failure that you may experience. It is easier to retreat to your comfort zone. But stop yourself and look for the opportunity to learn and grow from your experience. If you fail, you can start all over again. Henry Ford said, *"Failure is merely an opportunity to more intelligently begin again."*[7]

You have a choice to become the best school counselor or become the status quo of:

- "I can't."
- "That's too much work."
- "I'm too afraid to act alone."
- "I'd rather stay in my lane."
- "I do not want to cause any waves."

It is your choice. Who are you?

Are you willing to push through all the adversity in your school to make a difference? It is said that a redwood tree grows roots that are six feet deep. The roots wrap around other redwood tree roots for strength. A strong frame of mind rooted in the commitment to take action can keep the chain strong and less likely to break. Work with confidence, without complaining and arguing, and give it your very best in all that you do. Your willingness to remain strong and persistent will help you overcome your fears and place you on the road to success.

> *Whatever the mind can conceive and believe, it can achieve.*
>
> **Napoleon Hill**

The journey to a high-quality program begins with a powerful vision. However, to move beyond aspiration, a clear roadmap is essential. As a school counselor leader, you possess the capacity to bring your biggest dreams to life through intentional planning and unwavering belief in your abilities. Center your confidence in the knowledge that your leadership directly benefits your students. Dare to dream boldly and, more importantly, take decisive action to build those dreams into reality.

Transformational Leader

Leadership is a learned skill. Some school counselors naturally have these leadership skills, such as working successfully in a team, knowing the right time to approach an administrator, knowing how to organize a college or career fair, showing empathy toward grieving students, and much more. All these things are usually learned on the job. However, moving leadership to the next level entails *transformational* leadership, which is to empower leadership in others. The authors of *101 Solutions for School Counselors and Leaders in Challenging Times* write, *"This type of leadership, which capitalizes on an individual's strengths and collaborative staff member relationship styles, has led to shared governance, decision-making, leadership, data, and inquiry teams."*[8] Leadership is not easy, but it can be learned. It's about knowing how to involve others to help you successfully accomplish your program's goals. In other words, school counselors should not work alone but incorporate the help of others. The best leaders are followers of other great leaders. These leaders do not see themselves as "the buck stops here" authoritarians, but rather as a source of service to others. Leadership is not about a title or the amount of salary; it's about motivation, initiative, purpose, and inspiring others.

A transformational leader sees the big picture and inspires others by communicating and moving in the direction of a goal. They have additional qualities such as self-confidence, courage, a willingness to take risks, focus, determination, good moral character, and the ability to inspire others. Staff members will not follow a principal because of their title, but because they understand why the principal is working toward a particular goal. Such leaders are resilient and determined to stay focused on the greater cause. Many of these leadership qualities intertwine with one another, but there is a set of core beliefs within each of us that makes us who we are as leaders. A popular saying, sometimes attributed to Mark Twain, states, *"The two most important days in your life are the day you are born and the day you find out why."*

Simon Sinek, author of *Start with Why*, writes, *"It all starts from the inside out. It all starts with Why."* Sinek explains that all leaders must be ready to inspire others by articulating *why* they do what they do.[9] Examples of your "why" might be:

- Why do I want to be a school counselor?
- Why do I come to school every day?
- Why do I want to work with students?
- Why am I in education?

As a transformational leader, it is important to:

- **Find your *why*** and share ideas, give support, and inspire students, parents, and staff.
- **Believe and trust in yourself** to do the right thing, especially when you advocate for your students and your school counseling program.
- **Take action**, leaning into your *why* by attending conferences, reading, seeking advice from others, and knowing what works and what does not. Be a continuous learner.

We are all born with special gifts. We have ears to listen, eyes to see, hearts to feel, hands to touch, and brains to think. As leaders, we must incorporate all our senses when we problem-solve, think, plan, and inspire. I truly believe that if all decisions are made with students in mind, we can never be wrong. Our first priorities are to do no harm and educate students with fidelity, equity, and access for all. It takes a strong commitment for school counselor leaders to deliver the best school counseling program for all students. Do you have what you need to create the best possible school counseling program for all students? Let's start by discovering your qualities as a transformational leader.

TRANSFORMATIONAL LEADER REFLECTION

Discover the qualities you possess that make you unique as a transformational leader.

If a trusted friend were to describe who you are as a person, what would they say?

____

____

____

What would this friend say about your leadership skills? What qualities would they say that you possess?

____

____

____

Write out your *why* statement. Why am I a school counselor?

____

____

____

Write your vision statement.

To [write a leadership quality] so that [write your expectation/impact].

Example: To empower students and staff so that together they will all be successful.

To____so that

____

____

What will you do to increase your leadership role?

____

____

____

The Ripple Effect

A transformational leader has a ripple effect on people. Their actions have a way of inspiring others to make a positive difference. It's like throwing a pebble into the water and watching the ripples expand into more significant waves. You never know how your ripple can impact the lives of your students and other school counselors.

For example, have you ever run into a former student, and they tell you how much they appreciate you for what you did to help them get to where they are now? My students are now adults. As you know, they change a lot from high school. They are usually working adult mothers and fathers who come back and thank me for caring about them in their high school years. I run across them in various places (they usually recognize me first). Many of them go into detail to express how much they appreciate me as their former high school principal who cared enough about them to be by their side and advocate for their success.

It brings tears to my eyes that these former students will take the time to thank me. They often say how they remember when I helped or supported them. I'm amazed that what I thought was a small thing was impactful in their life at the time.

We may never fully grasp the far-reaching impact of our daily interactions – the hundreds of students we connect with, listen to, and support. Let the concept of the ripple effect be a persistent truth: each of us holds the potential to be the difference in a student's life. Our school environments are often characterized by their relentless pace and myriad demands, sometimes making sustained focus a challenge. Yet, within this whirlwind, what happens when that one student seeks our guidance? Is our default response, "I'm overwhelmed right now"? Or do we consciously choose to stop and prioritize their immediate need? Reflect on this: in that crucial moment, what action can you take?

I would often ask my school counselors to consider their lasting impression: "How do you aspire to be remembered by your students? Will their recollections be vague – 'that counselor who never smiled,' 'I never really knew my counselor' – or negative – 'I didn't feel comfortable talking to her,' 'He didn't seem to care about what I was going through'? Or will it be a comforting memory like, 'He always listened when I needed to talk'? Take a moment to truly reflect: what kind of school counselor do you want to be in the eyes of your students? What positive memories will they carry with them?

School counselors who make a difference in students' lives are usually extremely busy, knowing their students and their families. That is their top priority. Paperwork is important, but it is secondary in their minds. As you know, paperwork does not grow feet and leave your office; it will be there waiting for you tomorrow. However, a student will leave for the day, and that time and day with your student is gone.

To create a ripple effect that truly transforms students' lives, educators embody confidence, embrace calculated risks, foster teamwork, possess deep expertise, and genuinely value the human element. They rise to leadership roles and consistently model clear expectations for staff and students. These educators are powerful advocates for every student and collaborate effectively within and beyond school walls. Their willingness to lead is matched by their unwavering belief in and expert implementation of comprehensive school counseling programs, a mission they undertake with profound pride.

I remember when one of our high school counseling programs was struggling. They had a lead counselor, but she could not lead the group; there was in-house chaos. The administrator did not know what to do anymore with this dysfunctional team. Finally, one confident counselor became the change agent needed to make a difference in their school counseling department. She was fed up and bothered by the fact that nothing was getting accomplished, and that their reputation as school counselors was at stake. She was ready and willing to take the risk to go through the other school counselors' pushback and resistance. She led without the title of "lead counselor." As my team began to work with these counselors, we learned that they did not want to live in chaos but wanted a leader who would step up to the plate and lead. They wanted to be valued and appreciated, and were set to move to the next level. The counselor leader without a title was indeed an effective leader at heart and took pride in her work. Her desire to improve her school counseling program had a ripple effect on other counselors and elevated their program to the next level.

By the following school year, she became the titled lead counselor. Her team became successful with positive results, and their ability to work as a high-functioning team was commendable. I had them present their team accomplishments to other high school counselors, which made the ripple effect even greater. This is a perfect example of one person who had a ripple effect on their school counseling program, their school, and other counselors within the district. One brave decision shifted the entire counseling department. This ripple effect was powerful.

Take Action for Systemic Change

Some administrators don't want to know *what* you do, but *why* you do it. Then, you tell them *how* you will get the job done. Knowing the *why* is important, the key to convincing administrators that your mission and goals align with those of the school. In my experience as a principal, I liked it when counselors came to see me about a project they wanted to do. I especially enjoyed listening to them when they presented a written plan of why and how they were going to get the job done. I knew they had discussed it among themselves and needed my support or suggestions to carry the project forward. I was amazed when counselors took that much time to present a project that they put together to help students. I had no choice but to support them and get out of their way, because they were on a mission.

As a Director of Counseling Services, I believe that when a counselor wishes to accomplish a particular goal, they should make an appointment to show their administrator a written action plan that clearly lays out what they want to accomplish. This paints a clear path and specifies a direction for the project. Otherwise, the administrator is left to guess precisely what the counselor means to do.

The goal of any action you take to design your school counseling program is to serve students. This is your moment to shine and collaborate with others, such as the administrators, staff, or advisory council on how to implement your counseling program to help secure the academics and the well-being of all students. Your leadership is calling you to activate your action plan and encourage your stakeholders to follow and believe in your plan. If something does not work, change it and keep moving forward. Get the most out of your collaboration with others to make your quality school counseling program work for your students. Again, this all starts with your belief and vision for your school counseling program.

To increase the effectiveness of your leadership role, you must:

- **Be visible as often as you can:** Step out of your office during passing periods. Talk to your students during lunch periods.
- **Know your staff and the key role they play in your school:** Know which staff members are well-connected to the community and who you can count on for collaborative projects.
- **Know your community:** Establish your advisory council and present your mission and goals to the council.
- **Be the expert of your program:** Own the title as the expert in college/career, in social/emotional development, academic support, and organizing school-wide events.
- **Take on new challenges and push yourself:** All new opportunities are learning opportunities.

Effective leaders will create systemic change by believing in themselves and seeking help from others to make the necessary and positive changes needed for their schools, their students, and their school counseling programs. You can build your own circle of influence by using a working advisory council. Be strategic in your thinking and use your resources to their greatest advantage. Take the time to build your foundation, communicate, and train parents, staff, and community members about your school counseling program and its positive impacts.

Where do you want to go with your school counseling program?

What	What do you want to accomplish in your school counseling program?
Why	Why do you want to achieve this goal? Use data. (Most Important)
How	How will you achieve your goal? Step-by-step action plan
Who	Who can help you accomplish this goal? (Stakeholders)
Results	Did it make a difference? Let your administrator know the results of your school counseling program assessment.

How will you help your students succeed?

What	What do you want to help your students accomplish?
Why	Why is it important for students to accomplish this task? Why is it important to close gaps to student learning? (Equity & Access) Use data. (Most important)
How	How will you help remove barriers to student learning? Step-by-step action plan
Who	Who are your targeted students?
Results	How are your students different based on your efforts to help them succeed? Discuss the results with your administrator and advisory counsil.

Summary

It is important to know the *what*, *why*, *how*, *who*, and *results* of your school counseling program. If the results are successful, celebrate. If the results are not successful, learn from them, tweak them, and try again. Your business is about transforming yourself as a leader of a dynamic school counseling program and transforming student success. Believe in yourself and trust in your *why*.

CHAPTER 2

BRINGING YOUR LESSONS TO LIFE: EQUITY FOR ALL

Be the change you wish to see in the world.

Mahatma Gandhi

Equality versus Equity

The graphic above speaks to the difference between equality and equity. It demonstrates how some students need very little intervention because they have the resources needed to thrive, while others may need extra support to compete in our ever-changing society. One thing we cannot assume is that every student gets the same response and intervention. We must be flexible and adjust our programs and practices in ways that provide prevention for all and intervention for some as needed. If all students receive exactly the same services from school counselors, many will come up short. The school counseling program should be designed to meet the needs of all students at all levels.

The fundamental difference between equality and equity is paramount in today's Pre-K–12 educational landscape. While equality suggests providing every student with the same service, equity recognizes that all students require preventative measures, and some need more intensive interventions to achieve success. Equity, therefore, focuses on leveling the playing field by providing differentiated support based on individual needs. School counselors play a vital role in this by leveraging their professional expertise to understand the unique challenges students face. This understanding enables them to advocate effectively and determine the necessary level of intervention, ensuring all students have access to the high-quality resources they need to flourish academically, socially, and emotionally.

ADVOCACY

According to the Postsecondary National Policy Institute (PNPI), students who are the first to attend college in their family are more likely to face a myriad of financial, academic, and social barriers.[10] These barriers hinder their ability to earn a college degree and obtain a job with livable wages. Because these students are the first in their families to go to college, they do not have their parents' prior experience to lean on in difficult times. Many students enter college unprepared for the essential persistence and resilience required to navigate academic challenges and earn the degrees and qualifications necessary for meaningful careers.

Why is advocacy so important? School counselors are the heart of the school. Why? **Counselors are the only trained professionals on the campus who have been hired to be the number one advocate for students.** School counselors demonstrate advocacy best when they deliver a balanced, comprehensive school counseling program that promotes student achievement, social-emotional growth, and development.

Getting to Know Your Students

SCHOOL DATA PROFILE

So, what does advocacy look like? Number one, school counselors take the time to get to know their students. How? Counselors can get to know their students by understanding the demographic, academic, and socioeconomic makeup of their school populations. This information can be gathered by looking at demographic subgroups, academic and attendance outcome data, and other tools that help counselors gain a better understanding of the needs of their students.

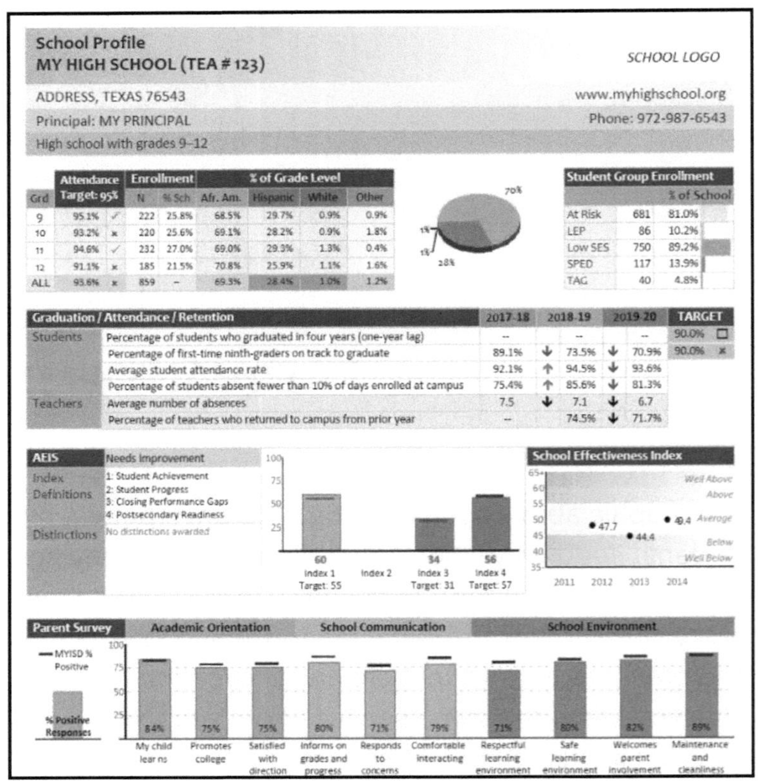

A school data profile, like the illustration below, gives counselors a holistic view of their student populations. It helps them plan and anticipate challenges students may face related to grades, assessments, attendance, and other student performance targets. School data profiles may also include teacher attendance and retention data and more.

NEEDS ASSESSMENTS

Feedback Surveys

Feedback surveys are a great advocacy tool for school counselors. Information collected from students, parents, staff, and other stakeholders gives counselors insight into ways they can design their school counseling programs to meet the academic, social-emotional, and personal needs of students. Data gathered from feedback surveys helps school counselors understand how their students think and behave. Feedback surveys also help school counselors understand the information parents need to support their child's learning process and educational experience.

Survey Tools

There are several survey tools counselors can use to collect quick, interactive responses. In the age of increased digital communication, school counselors can use tools like Google Forms, Survey Monkey, Zoom Polls, NearPod, Mentimeter, and others. These digital tools allow counselors to collect data that will help guide the direction of their training and instruction. They provide information school counselors need to develop the annual calendar of activities, to improve guidance and group instruction, and to use their time effectively each week to serve students. You can learn more about these tools by visiting these websites:

- **Google Forms:** forms.google.com
- **Mentimeter:** mentimeter.com/templates/poll-templates-examples/meetings
- **NearPod:** nearpod.com
- **Survey Monkey:** surveymonkey.com
- **Zoom Polls:** support.zoom.com/hc/en/article?id=zm_kb&sysparm_article=KB0066150

Below are examples of comprehensive surveys given at the beginning of the school year for stakeholders at the elementary and secondary levels.

ELEMENTARY FEEDBACK SURVEY

I am completing this survey as a:

- [ ] Student
- [ ] Parent
- [ ] School Staff Member
- [ ] Community Member

I am in/I have a student/I work with students in the following grade levels (check all that apply):

- [ ] Pre-K
- [ ] K
- [ ] 1st
- [ ] 2nd
- [ ] 3rd
- [ ] 4th
- [ ] 5th

School counselors help students with many concerns. Please tell us which topics are most important to you:

- [ ] Anger Management
- [ ] Resolving Conflict
- [ ] Decision-Making
- [ ] Study Skills/Making Good Grades
- [ ] Making Friends
- [ ] Self-Confidence/ Self-Esteem
- [ ] Coping with Stress and Anxiety
- [ ] College and Career

SECONDARY FEEDBACK SURVEY

I am completing this survey as a:

- [ ] Student
- [ ] Parent
- [ ] School Staff Member
- [ ] Community Member

I am in/I have a student/I work with students in the following grade levels (check all that apply):

- [ ] 6th
- [ ] 7th
- [ ] 8th
- [ ] 9th
- [ ] 10th
- [ ] 11th
- [ ] 12th

School counselors help students with many concerns. Please tell us which topics are most important to you:

- [ ] Coping with Stress and Anxiety
- [ ] Resolving Conflict
- [ ] Healthy Decision-Making
- [ ] Study Skills/Making Good Grades
- [ ] Self-Confidence/Self-Esteem
- [ ] College/Career Choice

Roadmap to Success

According to the Centers for Disease Control and Prevention, students make better decisions and experience better outcomes when they feel a sense of connectedness to the school. In other words, students learn better when they feel they are seen, heard, and valued as parts of their social environment. They want to know they are important.[11]

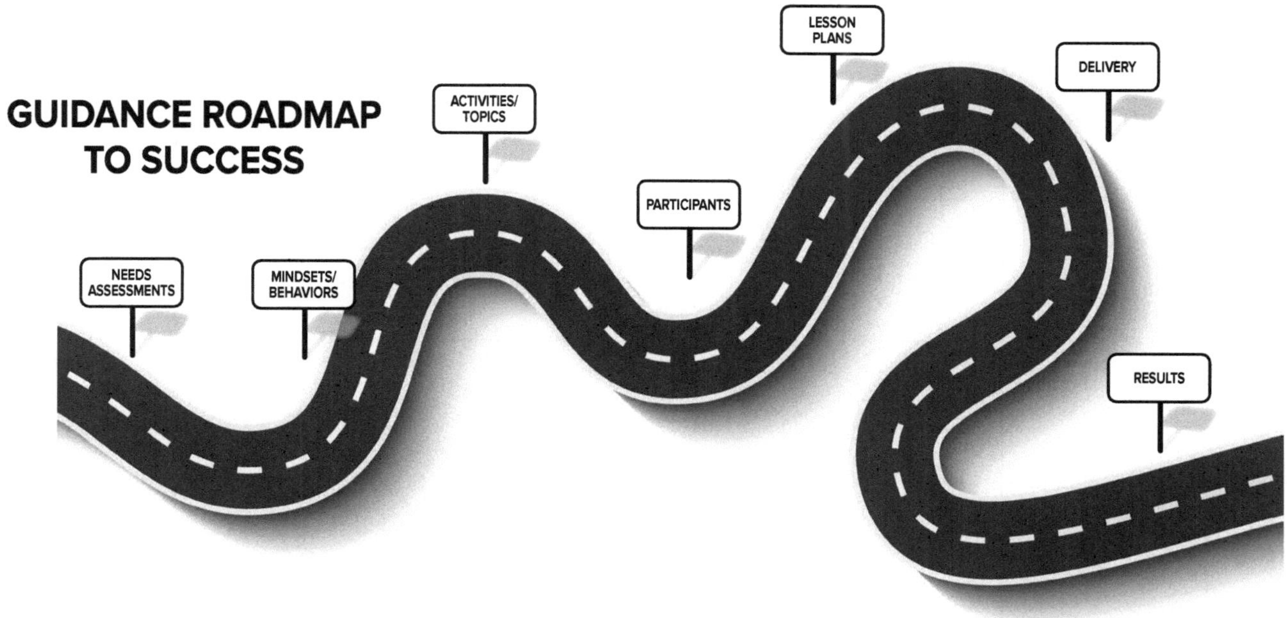

The Guidance Roadmap to Success is a visual illustration of how you can design your guidance lessons to help students achieve academic success, prepare for college and career, and develop appropriate social and emotional skills.

- **Needs Assessment:** First things first: start with a needs assessment to help you understand what your students know and don't know before teaching the lesson.
- **Mindsets and Behaviors:** Surveys conducted before the lesson help you understand the knowledge, attitudes, and skills students need to succeed using ASCA® (American School Counselor Association) Student Standards: Mindsets and Behaviors for Student Success (ASCA®, 2021).[12]
- **Activities/Topics:** Quality guidance lessons are great ways for students to get to know themselves and others. The activities you decide to employ with your students help them understand how to connect what they are learning in the guidance lesson to real-life situations. These activities should include an opportunity for every student to express themselves openly and authentically.
- **Participants:** It is important that the school counselor understands their audience. Each student group will present a need for a different approach, depending on its maturity level, verbal ability, and social-emotional needs. Knowing your audience is important for understanding how to address them.

LESSON PLANS, DELIVERY, AND RESULTS

The school counselor should design age-appropriate lessons to inform students and engage them in discussion about the topic at hand. It is important not just to present the lesson but to deliver it in such a way as to make it relevant and meaningful to students. In the end, the goal of any lesson is to affect student performance in a positive way.

GUIDANCE PLAN AT-A-GLANCE

DISTRICT OR STATE-MANDATED LESSONS						
SEL LESSONS (PRESENTED TO ALL CLASSROOMS)						
SCHOOL-WIDE AWARENESS DAYS						
AUGUST						
SEPTEMBER						
OCTOBER						
NOVEMBER						
DECEMBER						
JANUARY						
FEBRUARY						
MARCH						
APRIL						
MAY						

GUIDANCE PLAN AT-A-GLANCE (EXAMPLE)

DISTRICT OR STATE-MANDATED LESSONS	ORIENTATION TO COUNSELING	BULLYING PREVENTION	VIOLENCE PREVENTION	HEALTH & WELLNESS/SUICIDE PREVENTION	DRUG & ALCOHOL AWARENESS	COST OF COLLEGE
SEL LESSONS (PRESENTED TO ALL CLASSROOMS)	"Getting to Know You"	Be Kind	See Something, Say Something	Self-Care	Drug Education and Awareness	My College Dream
SCHOOL-WIDE AWARENESS DAYS	Back to School	Kindness Week	Taking Care of Us	Wellness Month	Red Ribbon Week	College Week
AUGUST	Classroom Guidance: K-6 "Getting to Know You"					
SEPTEMBER				Classroom Guidance: K-6 "Suicide Prevention"		College Fair
OCTOBER					School-wide Red Ribbon Week Campaign Classroom Guidance: K-6 "Drug Awareness"	
NOVEMBER		Classroom Guidance: K-6 "Bullying Prevention"				Classroom Guidance: K-6 "My College Dream"
DECEMBER				Classroom Guidance: K-6 "Self-Care"		
JANUARY	Classroom Guidance: K-6 "Making New Friends"					
FEBRUARY	National School Counseling Week	School-wide Kindness Week Campaign	Classroom Guidance: K-6 "Be Kind"			
MARCH	Guidance	Catch-up		Guidance	Catch-up	
APRIL	Guidance	Catch-up		Guidance	Catch-up	College Signing Day
MAY	Begin to end the school year and prepare to plan for next school year					Career Day

ASCA® LESSON PLAN (EXAMPLE)

AMERICAN SCHOOL COUNSELOR ASSOCIATION

Lesson Plan

School Counselor:	Tracey Brown
Lesson Plan Title:	"SELF-ESTEEM GROUP"
	☐ Single Classroom Lesson ☐ Unit of Classroom Lessons: Lesson _____ of _____ ☑ Small-Group Session Lessons: Lesson 1 of 4
Target Audience:	8th Grade Boys

Evidence Base:

☑ Best Practice *(commonly used and believed to be of high quality)*
☐ Action Research *(individual investigates own practice to improve content/delivery)*
☐ Research-Informed *(a review of research provides foundation for content/delivery)*
☐ Evidence-Based *(highest level of evidence, results published in peer-reviewed journal)*

ASCA Student Standards Targeted:		**Student Learning Objectives:**
Identify one or two student standards relevant for this targeted group and goal: *(Best practice = select one)*		For each of the selected student standards, write or select one or two learning objectives
M&B#	*Mindsets & Behaviors Statement*	*Student Learning Objectives*
M.4.	Self-confidence in ability to succeed	Student(s) will: Understand their individual strengths and culture
B-LS 7.	Long- and short-term academic, career and social/emotional goals	Create their 4-Year Plan and identify their career interests

Materials:

Online interest survey
Four-Year Plan template
Paper and pencil
Chart paper and markers

Describe how you will:

Updated, June 2021

To find the latest version of the ASCA® worksheets visit:
https://www.schoolcounselor.org/Recognition/RAMP/Templates.

ASCA® LESSON PLAN (EXAMPLE)

Introduce Lesson Topic/Focus:	Define self-esteem, culture, strengths, and career
Communicate the Lesson Objective:	Today's lesson will focus on understanding your strengths and how your culture plays a big part in who you are and what you can accomplish in life.
Teach Content:	Conduct a pre-test prior to the lesson to assess for students' level of self-confidence, career interests, and plan for the future. Discussion Questions: • Introduce yourself and tell us about your family • Name something unique about yourself and your culture • Describe what you would like to do in the future
Practice Content:	Create a K-W-L chart to identify what students know (K), what they want to know (W), and what they learned (L). Each student takes a turn answering the discussion questions. Counselor writes student responses on the K-W-L chart.
Summarize:	Review definition of self-esteem, culture, strengths, and career Have each student name one thing they have learned about another member of the group.
Close:	Thank students for being good listeners and for participating in the group. Summarize what students learned in the lesson. Inform students that next week's lesson will be focused on their interests, individual strengths, and future career.

Data Collection Plan – *For multiple lessons in a unit, complete this section only once for the unit.*	
Participation Data Plan: 8th Grade boys	
Anticipated number of students:	Eight students
Planned length of lesson(s):	30 minutes
ASCA Student Standards Data Plan:	
For each lesson/unit/small group, school counselors will administer pre-/post-assessment aligned with the selected ASCA Student Standards and student learning objectives. Pre-/Post-Assessment items are: 1. Pre-test administered before first lesson 2. Post-test administered after lesson (if standalone) or after last lesson of unit/group session 3. Pre/Post assessment attached	
Outcome Data Plan: (choose one and describe specific data point to compare)	
Examples: *Achievement: School counselor will compare reading levels of students before and after delivery of lesson.* *Attendance: School counselor will compare number of absences last year to this year.*	

Updated, June 2021

To find the latest version of the ASCA® worksheets visit: https://www.schoolcounselor.org/Recognition/RAMP/Templates.

ASCA® LESSON PLAN (EXAMPLE)

Discipline: School counselor will compare total number of disciplinary reports for peer-on-peer conflict first quarter with second quarter

☑ Achievement (describe): School counselor reviewed nine week grades for 8th grade boys who participated in group. The data showed 8th grade boys are underperforming on the 8th grade STAAR test by 20% in comparison to their peers. This small group was created to help improve students self-esteem and motivation to succeed in life and career.

☐ Attendance (describe):

☐ Discipline (describe):

Follow-Up Plans

Explain your plan for students who missed the lesson.

The school counselor will identify students who missed the session. A review will be conducted at the beginning of each session to ensure students receive the information they need to fully participate in group activities.

Explain your plan for students who did not demonstrate mastery on the pre-/post-assessment of student standards (M&B)/student learning objectives.

For students who do not demonstrate improved self-confidence in their ability to succeed, the school counselor will engage in one-on-one sessions to help students express their thoughts related to barriers that impede their progress.

Updated, June 2021

To find the latest version of the ASCA® worksheets visit: https://www.schoolcounselor.org/Recognition/RAMP/Templates.

USING DATA TO CLOSE GAPS

One of the best ways counselors ensure equity and access for students is by focusing on closing the gaps through small-group interventions. Using data can help counselors deliver meaningful lessons to change students' knowledge, skills, attitudes, and behaviors.

Tracking data is important to counselors' daily work. Data provides baseline information that identifies where students are and where they want to be. Data provides a pathway for counselors to develop intentional action plans that focus on healthy student development.

Understanding and utilizing data can sometimes feel like a hurdle, especially when so much of our work centers on the complexities of students' social-emotional well-being. Yet, how can we truly gauge the impact of our interventions without a way to track student progress? For instance, after facilitating a small group, how do we determine its effectiveness? And without examining our school data, how can we identify the specific gaps we need to address to better support our students?

Some students struggle and do not have the tools they need to manage their behavior in appropriate ways. This often leads to frequent discipline referrals that remove students from the classroom and cause a loss of instruction. When students lose instruction, their grades suffer, and they begin to experience huge knowledge gaps. When students experience a lack of knowledge, they become frustrated and seek opportunities to escape from the shame of not being able to do their work. They sit in the principal's office, counselor's office, or in in-school suspension settings, missing out on the very reason why they are there—to learn.

With no intervention, students are often left to figure things out on their own. They may not understand why they misbehave or what they need to do about it. They just know they are not able to do what is required in the class. Counselors have several tools in their toolkit to support students through very difficult situations. This is where data plays an important role in targeting and closing the gaps for struggling students. Take a look at the chart below.

- Can you determine what grade level has the greatest need in the second six-week period?
- What did the school counselor do to decrease the number of discipline referrals by the end of the third six weeks?

Discipline Referrals per Grade Level

Number of Referrals by Grade Level	6th	7th	8th	Total
Second Six Weeks Referrals	14	47	19	70
Third Six Weeks Referrals	13	24	12	45

Here's how the school counselor handled the situation:

The data report showed the 7th grade students had the highest number of discipline referrals for the second six weeks. After discussing his concern with the administrator, the school counselor found out that 40 percent of referrals came from students who were referred to the principal's office for bullying. The counselor understood that time away from class could cause enormous learning gaps for his students. He decided to collaborate with the 7th grade teachers to see if he could gain some insight into the increase in discipline referrals.

Based on feedback from teachers, the counselor decided to start a small group with twelve students with the highest number of discipline referrals to help them improve empathy and learn how to build positive relationships with other students. During his small-group sessions, the counselor used YouTube videos containing personal testimonials from students who had experienced bullying, recounting the great lengths they went to avoid confrontation with the bully, even to the point of attempting suicide. It was important for the counselor to help his students develop the ability to see life from another person's perspective and understand the emotional toll their behavior has on others. He also used role play to give students the opportunity to experience what it is like to be bullied. During the sessions, it was important for the counselor to listen to students and allow them to express their thoughts and feelings openly.

On the following pages is an example of the pre-assessment and post-assessment that demonstrates how the school counselor was able to use data to close the gap for students.

STUDENT PRE/POST ASSESSMENT

Name: ____ Date: ____________________

Circle your answer.

1. What do you do when you see someone being bullied?

   A. I help the victim.

   B. I walk away.

   C. I participate.

   D. I go and get help.

2. I can tell when others are feeling sad.

   A. Yes

   B. No

3. When I see someone sitting alone at lunch, I am more likely to...

   A. Invite them to sit with me and my friends.

   B. Make fun of them.

   C. Ignore them.

4. Do you know how to make new friends?

   A. No

   B. Yes

   If yes, please describe what you do to make new friends.

   ____

   ____

   ____

   ____

   ____

   ____

STUDENT PRE/POST ASSESSMENT RESULTS (EXAMPLE)

((Post-Assessment – Pre-Assessment) / Pre-Test) x 100 = % of Change

B-SS 4. Demonstrate empathy

1. What do you do when you see someone being bullied?

	Pre-Assessment	Post-Assessment	% Change
A. I help the victim.	2	9	250% Increase
B. I walk away.	7	0	100% Decrease
C. I participate.	1	0	100% Decrease
D. I go and get help.	2	3	50% Increase

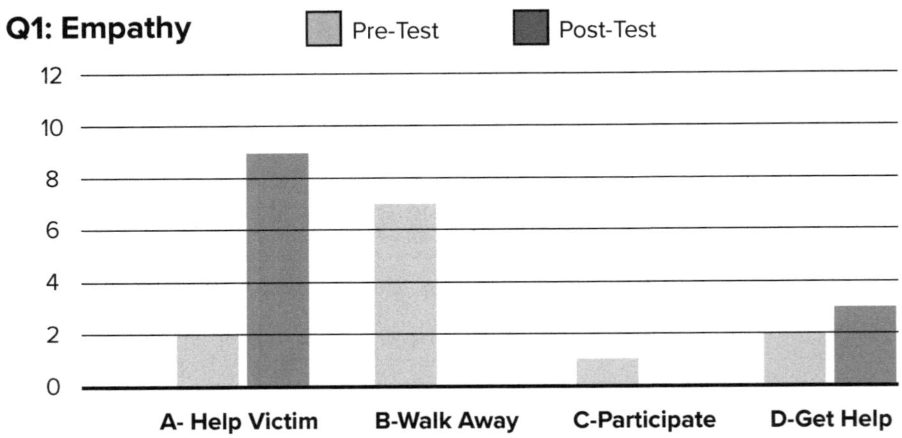

2. I can tell when others are feeling sad.

	Pre-Assessment	Post-Assessment	% Change
A. Yes	4	12	200% Increase
B. No	8	0	100% Decrease

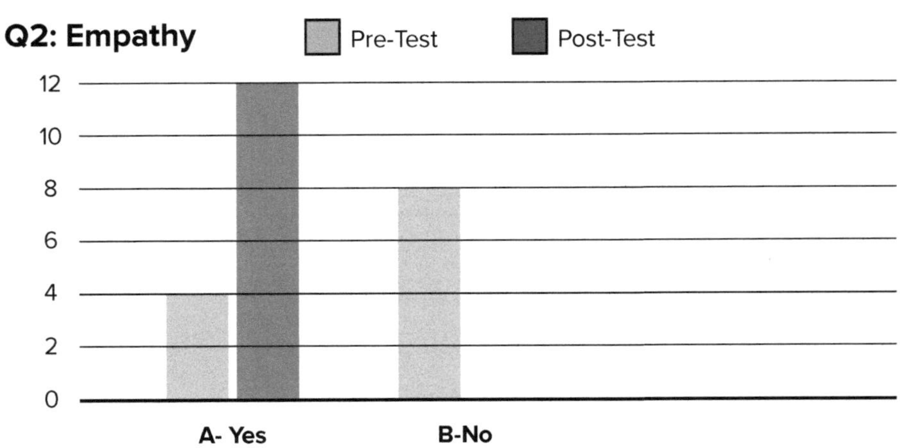

B-SS 2. Create positive and supportive relationships with other students.

3. When I see someone sitting alone at lunch, I am more likely to...

	Pre-Assessment	Post-Assessment	% Change
A. Invite them to sit with me and my friends.	1	10	900% Increase
B. Make fun of them.	2	1	100% Decrease
C. Ignore them.	9	1	90% Decrease

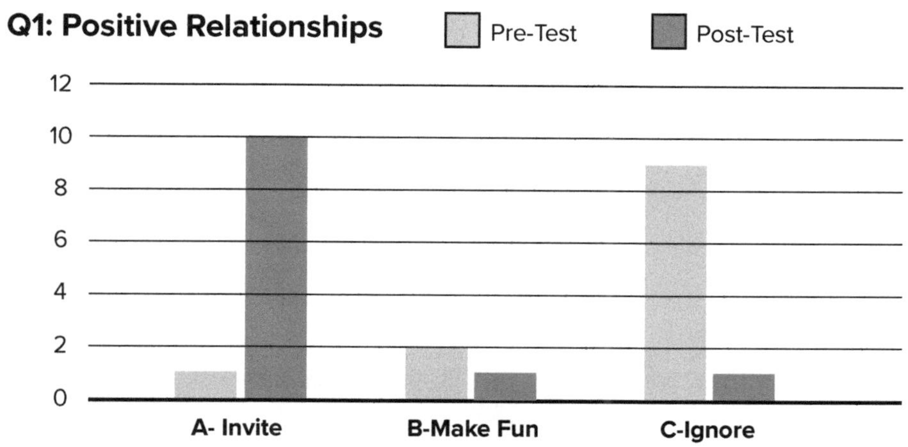

4. Do you know how to make new friends?

	Pre-Assessment	Post-Assessment	% Change
A. Yes	4	12	200% Increase
B. No	8	0	100% Decrease

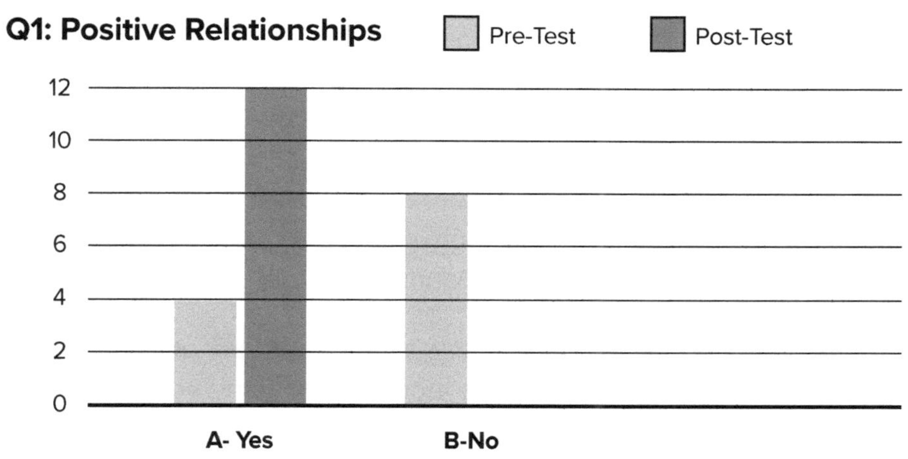

Student responses to "If yes, please describe what you do to make new friends."

- Before small-group interventions, one student stated they knew how to make new friends. He used words like giving someone a pencil, smiling at others, and sitting with a new student on the bus.
- After small-group interventions, eleven students were able to describe making new friends using words like saying hello to new people, inviting new students to sit with them for lunch, asking a new student if they need help, helping new students find their classroom, and giving a new student a friendly fist bump.

After reviewing the third six-week discipline report, the counselor noticed a 50 percent decrease in the number of 7th grade discipline referrals. He had the data to support the success of his small-group intervention. His students demonstrated the ability to show empathy and build positive relationships with others. As a result, students were able to remain in class, which improved their overall learning experiences. This is an example of how this school counselor was able to use data to identify and close gaps for students.

Annual Administrative Conference

ASCA® Annual Administrative Conferences are also a great way for school counselors to lead and advocate for students. Principals are the leaders of the school. They are charged with the task of ensuring that students are learning and developing in healthy ways. School counselors advocate for students and help remove any barriers that affect student learning. The amount of time counselors have to advocate for students depends on the principal-counselor relationship.

The Annual Administrative Conference is a formal meeting scheduled with the principal to discuss the priorities of the program, the roles and responsibilities of each member of the school counseling team, and the goals of the school counseling program. This is a great opportunity for counselors to have a voice and advocate for their school counseling programs. Some counselors fear they have no voice to make decisions about how they will carry out their counseling duties. The Annual Administrative Conference allows school counselors to discuss how they will spend their time working directly with and indirectly for students. It is important for counselors to emphasize the amount of time they need for program planning, committee assignments, and other counseling duties. In addition, this is also a time for counselors to make any budget requests for supplies and materials, identify members of their advisory team, discuss their calendar of events, and talk about professional development needs.

If the Annual Administrative Conference is carried out with fidelity, many of the barriers school counselors experience can be removed through an agreement concerning how the school counseling program will be managed throughout the year. School counselors must be intentional about planning, organizing, and delivering their conferences. It is best to discuss the principal's expectations for the program up front rather than become frustrated and function in a reactive mode all year long, which takes time away from students.

School counselors get buy-in from principals when they can show how they are making a positive impact on the academic, social, and emotional development of students. This is best accomplished when counselors can speak to the overall goals of the school and then identify target groups of students who can benefit from counseling interventions to close equity gaps and ensure student access to the resources needed to help them learn.

ASCA® ANNUAL ADMINISTRATIVE CONFERENCE (EXAMPLE)

AMERICAN SCHOOL COUNSELOR ASSOCIATION

Annual Administrative Conference

School Counselor **My Name** School Year **2024-2025**

After completing the school data summary, I have identified the following data priorities:
Middle school 8th grade boys are underperforming on the math state norm-referenced test by 15% in comparison to their female peers.

Based on these data priorities, I will address the following goals as listed in the annual student outcome goal plan templates:

Annual Student Outcome Goals	
1	To help improve academic performance in math for 8th grade boys by 3% from 68% to 71% passing.
2	

School Counselor Use of Time			
A minimum of 80% of time is recommended for direct and indirect student services and 20% or less in program planning and school support.			
Use of Time from Previous School Year ***Based on two use-of-time 5-day calculators from previous school year (attached)***			
Direct Student Services	Indirect Student Services	Program Planning and School Support	Non-School-Counseling Duties
30%	20%	25%	25%
Use-of-Time Plan for Current School Year ***Indicate your planned time allocations for this school year***			
Direct Student Services	Indirect Student Services	Program Planning and School Support	Non-Counseling Duties
50%	30%	20%	0%

Updated, June 2021

To find the latest version of the ASCA® worksheets visit: https://www.schoolcounselor.org/Recognition/RAMP/Templates.

ASCA® ANNUAL ADMINISTRATIVE CONFERENCE (EXAMPLE)

Ratio and Caseload

The American School Counselor Association recommended ratio is one school counselor per 250 students.

Ratio		One School Counselor	Per	_250___	Students
Caseload defined by:	☐	Alpha Assigned:	Last names beginning with:	_____ to _____	
	x	Grade Level:	Students in grades:	6-8	
	☐	All Students in Building			
	☐	Other: ______________________			

Program Implementation Plan to Address Priorities

Attach the following documents for review and discussion during the conference:

- Classroom and Group Mindsets & Behaviors Action Plan
- Closing-the-Gap Action Plan
- Annual Calendar

Advisory Council

The school counseling advisory council will meet to provide feedback and input on the school counseling program.

Fall Meeting Date:	September 15, 2024
Spring Meeting Date:	March 20, 2025
Proposed Members: *(names and stakeholder position)*	Include names of stakeholders and their positions here

Professional Development

I plan to participate in the following professional development based on annual student outcome goals and my School Counselor Professional Standards & Competencies self-assessment.

Date(s)	Topic	Cost
July 4-6, 2024	American School Counselor Association	$349
November 3-5, 2025	Lone Star State School Counselor Association	$155

Updated, June 2021

To find the latest version of the ASCA® worksheets visit:
https://www.schoolcounselor.org/Recognition/RAMP/Templates.

ASCA® ANNUAL ADMINISTRATIVE CONFERENCE (EXAMPLE)

School and District Committees and Professional Work		
Group	Time Commitment	School Counselor's Role
Student Support Team	1 hour/week	Member
Site-based Decision-making Team	1 hour/week	Member

Budget Materials and Supplies

Materials and supplies needed: Guidance Curriculum
IPADS

Annual budget: $ $5,000

School Counselor Availability/Office Organization

The school counseling office will be open for students/parents/teachers from 8:00 a.m. to 4:00 p.m.

My hours will be from 8:30 a.m. to 4:30 p.m. (if flexible scheduling is used)

The career center will be open from 9:00 a.m. to 3:00 p.m.

Other Staff and Volunteers

Role/Responsibility	**Person Assigned** (no signature required)
School Counseling Department Assistant	Ms. Janie Clark
Attendance Assistant/Clerk	Mr. Tom Day
Data Manager/Registrar	Mrs. Tana Jefferson
College and Career Center Assistant	
Assistant Principal	Mr. John Smith
Volunteers	Ms. Gabriela Marsh
Signatures of school counselor and administrator must be within the first two months of school.	
School Counselor Signature	*My Signature*
Administrative Signature	*Admin Signature*
Date Conference Held & Template Signed	September 15, 2024
First Day of School	August 13, 2024

Updated, June 2021

To find the latest version of the ASCA® worksheets visit: https://www.schoolcounselor.org/Recognition/RAMP/Templates.

DATA AND PRIORITIES USING THE ANNUAL ADMINISTRATIVE CONFERENCE

AMERICAN SCHOOL COUNSELOR ASSOCIATION **Annual Administrative Conference**

School Counselor **My Name** School Year **2024-2025**

After completing the school data summary, I have identified the following data priorities: Middle school 8th grade boys are underperforming on the math state norm-referenced test by 15% in comparison to their female peers.

Based on these data priorities, I will address the following goals as listed in the annual student outcome goal plan templates:

Annual Student Outcome Goals	
1	To help improve academic performance in math for 8th grade boys by 3% from 68% to 71% passing.
2	

An example of counselor advocacy for closing the gaps for student target groups might be to look at campus achievement data and identify learning gaps among your English/Language Learners (ELL). The data may show that these students are underperforming on achievement tests due to a lack of appropriate placement in courses that may help to improve their language acquisition skills. In this case, school counselors may work with administrators, teaching staff, and the LPAC (Language Proficiency Assessment Committee) to make sure students are properly identified and that their class schedules reflect the support they need to successfully master the language and content of the course. This is just one of many examples of how counselors use data to ensure that they have the amount of time they need to spend with and for struggling students to help close the gaps.

USE OF TIME

School Counselor Use of Time			
A minimum of 80% of time is recommended for direct and indirect student services and 20% or less in program planning and school support.			
Use of Time from Previous School Year ***Based on two use-of-time 5-day calculators from previous school year (attached)***			
Direct Student Services	Indirect Student Services	Program Planning and School Support	Non-School-Counseling Duties
30%	20%	25%	25%
Use-of-Time Plan for Current School Year ***Indicate your planned time allocations for this school year***			
Direct Student Services	Indirect Student Services	Program Planning and School Support	Non-Counseling Duties
50%	30%	20%	0%

The Annual Administrative Conference is a great way for school counselors to advocate for students. School counselors utilize this time to highlight the challenges students face based on outcome data. The school counseling team brings the data to the table and engages the principal in a discussion about the priorities for the year. More about program planning and organizing can be found below.

The counseling team will decide both the student outcome goals and how counselors will organize their time to meet those goals throughout the year. It is vital to be clear about the amount of time it takes to ensure every student's success. Counselors best serve students when they anticipate student challenges (rather than react to them) and plan for the time they need to deliver counseling services.

An evaluation of time spent with students is vital and must be a priority for school counselors. Students trust counselors who spend time with them and make them feel welcomed and supported. Therefore, counselors must plan their calendars so they can spend most of their time guiding, counseling, and advising students. The more time counselors spend with students, the less time they spend engaging in non-counseling duties. The Annual Administrative Conference should include a conversation between the principal and counselor to discuss the percentage of time counselors will need to deliver direct and indirect services to students, engage in program planning, and participate in fair-share activities that contribute to the overall success of the school.

RATIO AND CASELOAD

Ratio and Caseload				
The American School Counselor Association recommended ratio is one school counselor per 250 students.				
Ratio	One School Counselor	Per	_250___	Students
Caseload defined by:	☐ Alpha Assigned:	Last names beginning with:	_____ to _____	
	☒ Grade Level:	Students in grades:	6-8	
	☐ All Students in Building			
	☐ Other:			

Students come to us with varying needs and challenges. When the school counselor and principal agree on the goals for the year, the data helps them both to see which students need the most intensive intervention. Equity comes into play when counselors make specific plans to address student concerns school-wide and within their individual caseloads. It is important for the school counselor to understand which students they will serve individually and create plans to understand their counseling needs.

PROGRAM IMPLEMENTATION PLAN

When you have identified your priorities and set goals for closing the gaps, have a discussion with your principal about how you will address your students' needs throughout the year. The ASCA® Classroom and Group Mindsets and Behaviors Student Standards will help to drive this conversation. As you develop your annual calendar of events, discuss your plan for classroom guidance and small-group implementation. Your classroom guidance plan will ensure that all students receive instruction that helps improve their social-emotional learning as well as the knowledge and skills they need to succeed throughout the year.

Program Implementation Plan to Address Priorities

Attach the following documents for review and discussion during the conference:

- Classroom and Group Mindsets & Behaviors Action Plan
- Closing-the-Gap Action Plan
- Annual Calendar

Advisory Council

The school counseling advisory council will meet to provide feedback and input on the school counseling program.

Fall Meeting Date:	September 15, 2024
Spring Meeting Date:	March 20, 2025
Proposed Members: *(names and stakeholder position)*	Include names of stakeholders and their positions here

Planning for small-group implementation will also ensure that time is allotted for those students who need more intense attention to build relational and critical thinking skills. The **ASCA® Closing-the-Gap Action Plan** takes you back to the ASCA® Annual Student Outcome Goal Plan. This plan is an outline of how your team plans to address the targeted group of students who have been identified as a group that will receive intense school counseling intervention to help improve their achievement, attendance, or behavior outcomes.

As you set out to develop your annual calendar, you will do so with your classroom guidance, small-group, and ASCA® Closing-the-Gap Action Plan in mind. These items will be discussed throughout the remainder of this chapter.

ASCA® Classroom & Group Mindsets & Behaviors Action Plan

ASCA® Classroom and Group Mindsets & Behaviors Action Plan helps school counselors plan guidance activities designed to help students develop positive attitudes about themselves and their learning experiences in school. The example below is an illustration of a guidance plan that outlines activities counselors will deliver to their students through large-group/school-wide activities, small-group sessions, and classroom guidance lessons.

ASCA® CLASSROOM AND GROUP MINDSETS & BEHAVIORS ACTION PLAN (EXAMPLE)

Classroom and Group Mindsets & Behaviors Action Plan

The ASCA Student Standards: Mindsets & Behaviors for Student Success guide the planning and delivery of all student activities and interventions. The classroom and group Mindsets & Behaviors action plan provides an overview of the delivery of direct services in large group (LG), classroom (Class) and small-group (SG) settings. This plan presents the topics addressed, while the annual calendar presents the schedule of all classroom and groups activities.

Use the classroom and group Mindsets & Behaviors action plan to identify all ASCA Student Standards addressed through classroom and group activities. Although some activities address multiple standards, list the activity with the primary mindset or behavior addressed by the activity. It is not necessary to repeat activities with all standards addressed through that activity.

School Name	Date Created	Most Recent Revision Date
My School	4/1/2025	5/2/2025

Mindset Standards				
Mindset	**Activity/Focus or Purpose**	**Participants**	**Class/LG**	**SG**
M 1. Belief in development of whole self, including a healthy balance of mental, social/emotional and physical well-being				
M 2. Sense of acceptance, respect, support and inclusion for self and others in the school environment				
M 3. Positive attitude toward work and learning				
M 4. Self-confidence in ability to succeed	"My Dream in Life" Lesson	8th grade male students (8)		✓
M 5. Belief in using abilities to their fullest to achieve high-quality results and outcomes				
M 6. Understanding that postsecondary education and life-long learning are necessary for long-term success	Career Interest Survey	8th grade male students (8)		✓

Behavior Standards				
Learning Strategies	**Activity/Focus or Purpose**	**Participants**	**Class/LG**	**SG**
B-LS 1. Critical-thinking skills to make informed decisions	Stop, Think, Act – Study skills group activity	8th grade male students (8)		✓
B-LS 2. Creative approach to learning, tasks and problem solving				
B-LS 3. Time-management, organizational and study skills				
B-LS 4. Self-motivation and self-direction to learning				
B-LS 5. Media and technology skills to enhance learning				
B-LS 6. High-quality standards for tasks and activities				
B-LS 7. Long- and short-term academic, career and social/emotional goals	Self-Esteem	8th grade male students (8)		✓
B-LS 8. Engagement in challenging coursework				

To find the latest version of the ASCA® worksheets visit: https://www.schoolcounselor.org/Recognition/RAMP/Templates.

ASCA® CLASSROOM AND GROUP MINDSETS & BEHAVIORS ACTION PLAN (EXAMPLE)

B-LS 9. Decision-making informed by gathering evidence, getting others' perspectives and recognizing personal bias				
B-LS 10. Participation in enrichment and extracurricular activities				
Self-Management Skills	**Activity/Focus or Purpose**	**Participants**	**Class/LG**	**SG**
B-SMS 1. Responsibility for self and actions	Be Kind	All Levels (6-8)	✓	
B-SMS 2. Self-discipline and self-control				
B-SMS 3. Independent work				
B-SMS 4. Delayed gratification for long-term rewards				
B-SMS 5. Perseverance to achieve long- and short-term goals				
B-SMS 6. Ability to identify and overcome barriers				
B-SMS 7. Effective coping skills				
B-SMS 8. Balance of school, home and community activities				
B-SMS 9. Personal safety skills	Taking Care of Us	All Levels (6-8)	✓	
B-SMS 10. Ability to manage transitions and adapt to change				
Social Skills	**Activity/Focus or Purpose**	**Participants**	**Class/LG**	**SG**
B-SS 1. Effective oral and written communication skills and listening skills				
B-SS 2. Positive, respectful and supportive relationships with other students who are similar to and different from them				
B-SS 3. Positive relationships with adults that support success				
B-SS 4. Empathy	Self-Care	All Levels (6-8)	✓	
B-SS 5. Ethical decision-making and social responsibility				
B-SS 6. Effective collaboration and cooperation skills				
B-SS 7. Leadership and teamwork skills to work effectively in diverse groups				
B-SS 8. Advocacy skills for self and others and ability to assert self, when necessary				
B-SS 9. Social maturity and behaviors appropriate to the situation and environment				
B-SS 10. Cultural awareness, sensitivity and responsiveness	Making New Friends	All Levels (6-8)	✓	

To find the latest version of the ASCA® worksheets visit:
https://www.schoolcounselor.org/Recognition/RAMP/Templates.

ASCA® CLOSING-THE-GAP ACTION PLAN (EXAMPLE)

AMERICAN SCHOOL COUNSELOR ASSOCIATION

Closing-the-Gap Action Plan/Results Report

School Name	**MY SCHOOL**
Annual Student Outcome Goal	By May 2025, math scores for 8th grade boys will increase by 3% from 68% to 71%.

ASCA Student Standards (Limit of two standards)

1. M 6. – Understanding that postsecondary education and lifelong learning are necessary for long-term success.
2. B-LS 1. Critical-thinking skills to make informed decisions.

Mindsets & Behaviors Pre-/Post-Assessment Statements (Rating Scale: 0-100%)

1. I feel good about my ability to achieve.
2. I know how to ask for help.
3. I understand the role education will play in helping me achieve lifelong success.
4. I am confident in myself.

Interventions That Support Achieving the Annual Student Outcome Goal

Describe Direct Student Services (minimum of two)	Describe Indirect Student Services (minimum of two)
1. Classroom Guidance – Career Pathways 2. Small Group Counseling – 8th grade boys (math)	1. 2 Parent meetings (Focus: Supporting Your Child's educational journey and Parent Resources) 2. Serve on Multi-Tiered System of Support (all counselors)

Systemic Focus

Identify school or system policies, procedures or practices that create or maintain inequities relevant to this goal.

1. We have noticed discipline referrals increased last year due to incidences involving cell phones.
2. Students are having difficulty understanding how to advocate for themselves and ask for help from an adult in the school, instead of using social media to handle problems.

List one or two strategies that could influence systemic change related to this goal.

Minimize time missed from class by evaluating the cell phone policy in the school. We believe teaching students how to manage cell phone use during class will help improve their learning experience and academic performance overall.

To find the latest version of the ASCA® worksheets visit: https://www.schoolcounselor.org/Recognition/RAMP/Templates.

ASCA® CLOSING-THE-GAP ACTION PLAN (EXAMPLE)

AMERICAN SCHOOL COUNSELOR ASSOCIATION

Closing-the-Gap Action Plan/Results Report

Baseline Data	Results Data
Participation Data Plan	**Participation Results Data**
Anticipated Our goal is to conduct a group for eight 8th grade boys.	*Actual* All eight students participated in each small group session.
Mindsets & Behaviors Pre-Assessment Results	**Mindsets & Behaviors Post-Assessment Results**
Pre-Assessment Data *(calculate the average student response for each item)* 1. I feel good about my ability to achieve. (40%) 2. I know how to ask for help. (30%) 3. I understand the role education will play to help me achieve lifelong success. (40%) 4. I am confident in myself. (25%)	*Post-Assessment Data* *(calculate the average student response for each item)* 1. I feel good about my ability to achieve. (80%) 2. I know how to ask for help. (60%) 3. I understand the role education will play to help me achieve lifelong success. (80%) 4. I am confident in myself. (60%)
Outcome Data Plan	**Outcome Data Results**
Baseline Data: In 2024, math scores for 8th grade boys were 68%.	*Final Data:* In 2025, math scores for 8th grade boys were 73%. *Percent Change: 5%*

Reflection

- How did the interventions facilitate the attainment of identified ASCA Student Standards?
  With a focus on the 8th grade boys, the small group intervention was effective in teaching them how to increase their self-confidence by working together and improving their ability to ask questions when needed.

- How could the interventions be improved (e.g., consider timing, number and type of services, student access and identified barriers)?
  Due to the success of the small group intervention, we would like to conduct additional small groups to help improve self-confidence and the students' ability to ask for help.
  Create additional time for follow-up with the small group to ensure that they are successful throughout the year and to provide ongoing support.

To find the latest version of the ASCA® worksheets visit: https://www.schoolcounselor.org/Recognition/RAMP/Templates.

Annual Calendar

The annual calendar drives the flow of your school counseling program. It is a powerful tool you can use to ensure that the needs of all students in your school are addressed throughout the year. The annual calendar helps you stay on track from month to month to ensure that the big-ticket items are accomplished. It is also a great tool to help you plan your weekly calendar of activities for a balanced, comprehensive school counseling program.

Building the annual calendar of events not only serves the purpose of prioritizing school counseling activities; it also helps to identify other campus priorities as communicated by the principal or campus administrator. In this way, you are not functioning in a silo. Instead, you are making sure your school counseling activities align with the priorities of the campus. The annual calendar helps to ensure that the principal and counseling team are all on the same page and moving in the same direction. It is best practice that the annual calendar is developed and discussed before the school year starts. As circumstances arise throughout the year, the calendar can always be adjusted to meet the needs of your students and campus.

Below is an example of an **Annual Calendar** using the ASCA® template. It serves as a roadmap to your time management schedule. The annual calendar helps you set priorities for delivering direct and indirect services. In addition, the annual calendar will help you plan for school support throughout the year.

AMERICAN SCHOOL COUNSELOR ASSOCIATION

Annual Calendar Template

School: **MY MIDDLE SCHOOL** Academic Year: **2024-2025**

A minimum of 80% of time recommended for direct and indirect student services and 20% or less in program planning and school support

	Delivering		
Month	**Direct Student Services Activities** *(Include dates of school counseling initiatives or events, classroom and group activities, career or college nights, schoolwide academic support events, etc.)*	**Indirect Student Services Activities** *(Significant collaborations, leadership and advocacy activities)*	**Program Planning and School Support** *(Defining, Managing, Assessing, Fair-Share Responsibilities)*
Ongoing Services	Guidance Curriculum Instruction Individual Counseling Small Group Counseling Appraisal and Advisement sessions		School Counseling department meeting (every Monday at 3:00pm) Monthly Leadership meetings Monthly Data Review meetings
August		Open House for all students	Professional Development compliance training
September	Counseling Orientation guidance lessons	Advisory Council meeting Districtwide Back-to-School parent meetings	District School Counselor meetings
October	***Small group counseling for 8th grade boys to help improve math scores***		Red Ribbon Week Drug and Alcohol Prevention and Awareness Month
November			LSSSCA Conference
December	Small group: Study Skills	District Vertical Team Meetings	District School Counselor meetings
January	Career Interest guidance lesson (Gr. 6,7,8)		
February	Violence Prevention: Teen Dating Violence Course Selection guidance lesson (Gr. 6,7,8)		District School Counselor meetings
March	Graduation Plan/Endorsement guidance lessons (Gr. 8)	Advisory Council Meetings	
April			
May	College-Career Fair Student Transition plan lessons		Final District meetings Prep for ASCA conference in July
June			

Updated, June 2021

To find the latest version of the ASCA® worksheets visit:
https://www.schoolcounselor.org/Recognition/RAMP/Templates.

Advisory Council

Another way school counselors can advocate for students is through an advisory council. We know that students learn best when all stakeholders are on the same page, seeking positive results for students. An advisory council is a great way for school counselors to join with a team of stakeholders to receive feedback and discuss ways they can work together to get positive outcomes for students.

Advisory council meetings are held two to three times per year. The meetings are led by all members of the school counseling team. The team invites administrators, teachers, staff, parents, students, and community members to the advisory council meeting. These meetings are held to discuss the vision and mission of the school counseling program, the school data profile, results of the campus needs assessments, and the Annual Student Outcome Goal Plan. The school counseling team also asks members of the team for suggestions on how to design their counseling activities to meet the needs of students.

The second advisory council meeting is typically held mid-year to discuss the progress of the school counseling program and accomplishments from the first semester. This is also a time when the advisory council may provide feedback on the counseling program and make suggestions for the spring semester.

A final advisory council meeting may be held at the end of the year. At this meeting, advisory council members discuss and evaluate the outcomes of the school counseling program and make suggestions for the following year.

Below is an example of the **Advisory Council Meeting Agenda** and **Advisory Council Meeting Agenda Minutes**.

A review of data helps counselors identify priorities and set their program goals for the year. Discussing those goals with administrators and the advisory council helps counselors develop their guidance plans. Counselors should develop their guidance plans based on the mindsets and behaviors identified for groups of students in the school to help promote academic achievement and social-emotional well-being. An advisory council may be your best advocate in the school.

ASCA® SCHOOL COUNSELING ADVISORY COUNCIL AGENDA (EXAMPLE)

AMERICAN SCHOOL COUNSELOR ASSOCIATION

School Counseling Advisory Council First Semester Agenda

School:	My School	Meeting Date/Time:	9/15/24
School Counseling Program Vision Statement: All students can achieve.			
School Counseling Program Mission Statement: To provide high quality school counseling services for all students.			
Annual Student Outcome Goals *(list all)*: To improve math achievement for 8th grade male students by 3% from 68% to 71%.			

Agenda Items (at minimum)	School Counselor Facilitating Discussion
I. Welcome & Introduction	School Counselor A
II. School Data Summary	School Counselor B
III. Action Plans Discussion/Feedback • Annual Student Outcome Goal Plan • Classroom and Group ASCA Mindsets and Behaviors Action Plan • Closing-the-Gap Action Plan	All members
IV. Closure	School Counselor C

The Next Meeting of the Advisory Council is planned for:	March 15, 2025

Updated, June 2021

To find the latest version of the ASCA® worksheets visit: https://www.schoolcounselor.org/Recognition/RAMP/Templates.

ASCA® SCHOOL COUNSELING ADVISORY COUNCIL MINUTES (EXAMPLE)

School Counseling Advisory Council First Semester Minutes

School:	My School	Meeting Date:	9/15/24
Meeting Start Time:	3:00 p.m.		
Members Present/Stakeholder Position:	School Counselor A School Counselor B School Counselor C Teacher Parent Assistant Principal		
II. School Data Summary			
Minutes: The committee reviewed the School Data Profile and noticed math scores for students in the school are below the state average on the state, norm-referenced test.			n/a
III. Action Plans			
Annual Student Outcome Goal Plan(s) Minutes: The committee noticed 8th grade boys in the school saw the largest gap scoring 15% below the average on the math state exam.			Counselor B Will take the lead to identify 8th grade boys who may benefit from group counseling to improve self-esteem and self-confidence.
Classroom and Group Mindsets & Behaviors Action Plan Minutes: The team discussed ways they can provide students with opportunities to obtain the knowledge and skills needed to improve self-confidence in their ability to achieve.			Counselors, Parents, Assistant Principal, Parent
Closing-the-Gap Action Plan(s) Minutes: The results of interventions will be addressed in the March 2025 meeting.			All
Next Meeting Date/Time:	March 15, 2025		

To find the latest version of the ASCA® worksheets visit: https://www.schoolcounselor.org/Recognition/RAMP/Templates.

PROFESSIONAL DEVELOPMENT

According to the American School Counselor Association (ASCA®), the most important asset school counselors can give students is their time. School counselors work diligently every day to ensure their students' success. As we strive to advocate on behalf of our students, we must realize that the world is constantly changing.

There are many questions concerning how we help our students develop in times of crisis. As school counselors, how do we respond to this kind of challenge? How do we continue to advocate for our students and support them through academic and social limitations? How do we connect our students to peers so they can learn to build healthy relationships and resolve conflict in peaceful ways? How do we ensure equitable practices and access to quality education for those students who need more intense support?

Now more than ever, school counselors must be intentional about how we engage our students and support them through these troubling times. Even more so, we need to find new ways to embrace our students and ensure they feel loved, supported, and positive about their future outcomes. School counselors must be open to learning and growing to help students meet the challenges of our day.

In 2019, I had the amazing opportunity to become a counseling director for a large urban school district. As I approached this new opportunity, it was very important for me to adopt a model that had a track record of supporting student success. My goal was to assist our school counselors with the tools necessary to implement a comprehensive guidance and counseling program geared toward closing the equity and access gaps for all students. To accomplish this task, I needed to rely on a proven model based on research and best practices, which was the *ASCA® National Model: A Framework for School Counseling Programs* (4th Edition).[13]

Our students are valuable to us. It is our responsibility to help them reach their highest potential, realize their strengths, and learn from their challenges. We want our students to know who they are and understand the benefits of education to live a great quality of life. It is to this end that school counselors are essential to the very fabric of their schools.

For many years, professional school counselors were often tasked with providing ancillary services. However, as needs have changed and our profession has grown, school counselors have come to be recognized as an essential part of student success.[14] Why? Because their goal is to remove barriers to student learning and to promote postsecondary success. School counselors' goals are now integrated into the fabric of the school. Educators now recognize that students cannot learn if they are constantly having to deal with high academic demands, violence, suicide, peer pressure, institutional racism, sexism, homelessness, drug use, and more. Now more than ever, school counselors are needed in schools to teach students effective coping strategies for dealing with stress, anxiety, anger, and sadness. School counselors are also essential to help students achieve their educational goals and prepare for life after high school.

As school counselors, it is essential for us to increase our knowledge and skills related to removing barriers for students. We must continue to stay abreast of research and best practices in our field to deal with the challenges our students face. As I recall the challenges of COVID-19, several counselors were faced with trying to figure out how to serve students virtually and meet their basic needs. School counselors were faced with several questions, such as "How do we maintain confidentiality while counseling with students virtually?" "How do we use technology to connect with students?" and "How do we connect our students to social services needed for survival?" All of these challenges led us to problem-solve together and lean on professional organizations and best practices to meet our students' needs.

SCHOOL COUNSELING ORGANIZATIONS

We give thanks to our national, state, and local school counseling organizations for helping guide us through this unique challenge. They became a great way to collaborate with other school counselors to get the latest ethical, legal, and professional practices that helped guide our work in schools. It gave us a roadmap for dealing with the crisis at hand.

Many state organizations host annual conferences where school counselors can learn best practices to help improve their skills in counseling, advising, collaboration, coordination, and consultation. They may also provide the latest information released from state legislatures that outlines the work school counselors do with students. In some states, there are regional educational service centers that offer professional development sessions to help counselors build their knowledge and skills in college and career readiness and social-emotional development. Many professional school counselor organizations also have award recognitions that can serve as great ways for school counselors to inform their colleagues and stakeholders of the amazing work they do for students.

Summary

Throughout this section, we have outlined how a counselor's intentional approach to identifying the needs of their students is an absolute must to ensure the success of all students. A program design that is based on a vision of success for all students and intentional analysis of data to address gaps in achievement, attendance, and discipline is how we ensure equity and access for all students. Purposeful planning of our annual calendar helps to protect our time to serve students. Training and professional development are also critical to ensure that we learn and grow to meet our students' needs. When we are intentional about our work and our school counseling program, we can ensure equity and access for all students.

CHAPTER 3

IT'S MOMENTS, NOT MINUTES: EFFECTIVE TIME MANAGEMENT STRATEGIES

Time is a choice; it can either be wasted or invested.

Grant Cardone

Managing Work in a Chaotic World

Effective school counselor leaders recognize that time is not just a resource; it's a finite and irreplaceable asset. Once spent, it's gone. Understanding this urgency drives leaders to make conscious choices about how they allocate their time. While we can't accumulate time, we can strategically invest it. While the workload will always be there, proactive planning and thoughtful time management are essential for impactful leadership. Consistent planning allows us to tackle even the most overwhelming tasks with a focused, step-by-step approach.

When you prepare and plan your weekly calendar in a consistent fashion, you are planning for success. Find out your best time and place to plan. Planning does not happen automatically. It is something that you must develop a habit of doing. If you are consistent about the time spent in planning, you can effectively form a habit. This habit, repeated enough times, will become automatic. Ed Foreman writes, *"Good habits are hard to form but easy to live with. Bad habits, on the other hand, are easy to form but hard to live with."*[15] Be kind to yourself as you intentionally plan and balance work and family. The time you spend on planning will help you save time and energy because you know where you are going and what needs to get done. Planning gives you a guided path and direction to move forward. You may be thrown off the path, temporarily, but you can get back on track much more easily with a solid plan.

There is an 80/20 Rule when thinking of your day. According to ASCA®, the 80/20 rule means that a minimum of 80 percent of a school counselor's time should be spent on direct and indirect student services.[16] The majority of your time should be spent meeting *with* or *for* students through direct or indirect services. The students are in school for a short period of time, and we must take advantage of meeting students individually, in small groups, or in classrooms. School counselors must concentrate their work on designing and delivering a school counseling program that will impact positive student outcomes. The students are and must be our number one focus. An example of the **Use-of-Time 5-Day, 80/20 calendar** can be found on the ASCA® website at https://www.schoolcounselor.org/Recognition/RAMP/Templates.

According to Pamela Vaccaro, another strategic planning idea related to the 80/20 time management rule is a concept known as the "Pareto Principle," developed by an Italian economist, Vilfredo Pareto, in 1895. He believed, *"... that 80 percent of your results come from 20 percent of your activities."*[17] In other words, if you add ten things to do to your daily schedule, only two of those activities will be worth more than the eight activities listed. As humans, we tend to do the fun and easy stuff first. The most challenging and thought-provoking activities take more effort and sometimes are set aside for another day.

We must learn to discipline ourselves to focus on completing the most important activities first, the ones that add value to our time, such as conducting small groups, meeting with individual students, conducting classroom guidance lessons, etc. Most school counselors value time spent with or for students; however, some activities are derailed by insignificant tasks. Be aware not to fall victim to these constraints. They will keep you from doing and achieving your school counseling program responsibilities. Be fierce and push through your day. Every moment counts.

ASCA® also believes that no more than 20 percent of a school counselor's time should be spent in program planning and school support activities. Managing your school counseling program is very important. Finding an organized way of controlling the traffic in your office, your daily calendar, responding to emails or texts, the needs of your administrators, and all other duties as assigned is extremely challenging for school counselors. There is hope in maintaining your sanity as you attempt to organize and plan your year, your month, and your day. Don't forget to communicate and share your calendar, either by posting a weekly calendar outside your office door or emailing it to your staff.

Celebrate when you have completed an entire week on your calendar that you intentionally and faithfully planned. Feel good about your accomplishments. Embrace your success with joy and be a gift to yourself and others.

Here are my top eight rules for time management. Thoughtful time management is a tool for self-improvement and stress reduction:

1. Respect the limits of time.
2. Include time for family, friends, leisure, and dreams.
3. Accomplish something on your plan every day.
4. Evaluate and revise your plan frequently.
5. Carry your calendar with you at all times. This may include print or electronic devices.
6. Recognize that time management is pre-planning.
7. The best time management is individual. Figure it out.
8. Time management is stress management. Take charge of your use of time and change negative stress into a sense of accomplishment.

The School Counselor Time Management System

THE ELEPHANT IN THE ROOM

Given the multifaceted demands on school counselors – from annual program planning to daily student interactions – effective time management isn't just a skill; it's a necessity for sustainable practice. Without intentional organization, the various responsibilities can quickly become overwhelming. Recognizing the finite nature of our time, particularly the limited moments we have to connect with students each day, underscores the importance of strategic planning. Time, once elapsed, is irretrievable. That's the elephant in the room. Therefore, mastering time management is crucial for school counselors to not only serve their students effectively and implement a comprehensive program but also to navigate urgent situations and fulfill all assigned duties with intention and impact.

Successful planning is not about getting more activities done in a day but about getting the most important things done well. It is important to use a daily planner that works for you. A daily planner can be customized just for your needs. Using one calendar instead of multiple calendars can be a more effective way of planning your time. Keep it simple and easy.

As a former counseling director of a large urban school district with a total of 400 school counselors at all levels, I had to figure out a way to manage my time effectively and efficiently.

By knowing how to manage my time wisely, I felt less pressured when faced with deadlines. I felt more control over my time, and I felt better about myself at the end of the day.

The rewards of good planning save you time and effort. It leaves very little room to waste. During each well-planned week and day, you will be better able to free yourself to make decisions, avoid frustration, handle crises, manage stress, and keep from getting bogged down with other people's agendas. I would caution you not to overschedule or create a schedule that's too rigid. Give yourself enough time in the day to deal with unexpected interruptions. It is a good idea to leave room in your schedule for planning and preparing lessons for your students.

These are my top five tips for planning my school counseling program:

1. Plan...Plan...Plan
2. Plan with an Annual Calendar
3. Use *Stomp It Out! Tasks*
4. Plan weekly
5. Plan daily

Five Tips for Planning Your Work

TIP #1: PLAN...PLAN...PLAN.

Make it a habit to plan your year, your week, and your day. According to James Clear, author of *Atomic Habits: An Easy Way to Build Good Habits & Break Bad Ones*, *"A habit is a routine or behavior that is performed regularly and, in many cases, automatically."*[18] You get what you repeat until it becomes part of your habit of planning. The task of building a good habit is like eating the elephant in the room, one bite at a time. Figure out what works for you. Your commitment to your plan will lead to your progress. Stick with it and don't give up.

You are the only one who can control your time. We all work hard, but work smarter, not harder. Working hard on the wrong tasks can lead to frustration, not progress. Focus on the tasks that need to be done and prioritize. When we were teachers, we had to take time to plan lessons for our students. Guess what? As school counselors, we must do the same. Make time to plan and build your own weekly calendar. This will drive your daily calendar. This calendar, in turn, will drive your sense of priority concerning what needs to be done by the end of the day or the end of the week. Make it a must to develop a weekly planning ritual. For example, my planning time is every Sunday evening. I will have my annual calendar and my Stomp It Out! Task list as I build my weekly and daily calendar. This gets me ready to start my new week. You can choose any day of the week to plan but make it the same time and the same place. Make it your time to think and plan for the week. At the end of the week, you will have evidence of all the hard work accomplished that week. Congratulations!

TIP #2: PLAN WITH AN ANNUAL CALENDAR.

This is the big picture for the school year. The annual calendar maps out all the specific activities that need to be accomplished within the year that are coordinated or led by you or your counseling team. An annual calendar used in a monthly format is the framework of your school counseling program. Know the activities that must be completed for each month. Some of the activities may include Career Week, Red Ribbon Week, FAFSA month, back-to-school night, suicide awareness, bullying prevention month, etc. The annual calendar is a good way to share with all stakeholders about the upcoming activities for the year or the month. The development of the annual calendar is a team effort that should be shared with all major stakeholders, which should include your advisory council. Sharing your calendar is also a great way to advocate for the time you need to deliver your school counseling program.

TIP #3: PLAN TO USE *STOMP IT OUT! TASKS.*

Before moving on to the weekly schedule, develop a strategy for keeping up with the information you receive from day-to-day and week-to-week. The *Stomp It Out! Tasks* are an ongoing list of tasks you may receive at a meeting that you can jot down and prioritize throughout the week. Your *Stomp It Out! Tasks* are an ongoing plan. You can add a task to your calendar, along with a timeline for completion. The *Stomp It Out! Tasks* are new items given to you by someone else from a team meeting or by an administrator, etc. When writing the task, include the deadline and add it to your calendar. You can carry over any tasks from the prior week that were not completed. Use this *Stomp It Out! Task* list when you plan for the week to make sure you haven't forgotten any important due dates. When a task is completed, check it off. This gives you a great sense of accomplishment and helps you keep up with all your assigned tasks. You will find an example of the ***Stomp It Out! Tasks*** in the following pages.

TIP #4: PLAN WEEKLY.

Use your annual calendar and your *Stomp It Out! Tasks* when you prepare for your week. Add the items, with time slots of activities, to be completed that week. Your weekly calendar may include class guidance, small groups, leadership meetings, district meetings, MTSS meetings, individual counseling, parent meetings, etc. It is important to have a calendar with time slots to give you a picture of how much time you have on a specific day and to see all the items to accomplish by the end of the week. For activities not completed on a specific day, you can draw an arrow or use another symbol to indicate that you have moved an item to the following day. If you do not have room to add for the next day, add it to your *Stomp It Out! Task* list to complete at the earliest time available. Remember, do not cross off any activity/task from your *Stomp It Out! Tasks* list until it has been completed.

TIP #5: PLAN DAILY.

Use your weekly calendar to focus on each specific day of that week. Plan your daily activities by listing everything you need to do that day, either by a chunk of time or a specific time/appointment. List any priorities that must be done from the *Stomp It Out! Tasks*. Don't forget to allow time in your calendar for interruptions, filing, returning phone calls or emails, crisis plan follow-up, etc. If you are not able to follow your schedule for that day, that's OK. Just move everything to the next day or add items to the *Stomp It Out! Tasks* as a reminder of things that must be done the next day or the next week. Do not ignore any items on your calendar, especially when they involve students who are expecting you. Canceling sessions with your students can be a real letdown for them. If you get off track, accept it and get back on track. Do not agonize over it.

At the end of the week, reflect on what went right with your calendar, what needs to change, what distractions held you back, and, of course, celebrate your successes. Keeping a written journal of your learning and your accomplishments will help you better control your day, manage distractions, and use your time effectively and wisely.

This plan allows YOU to control your day!

Take time to plan by keeping the same time and the same place.

If you say, *I don't have time to plan*,
it puts your day in charge of you,
rather than you in charge of your day.

It's the elephant in the room, take it one bite at a time.

You can do it!

Procrastination

Author Brian Tracy writes, "*Procrastination is not only the thief of time; it is the thief of life.*"[19] Think about that statement. The more you procrastinate; the more time is wasted on little to nothing. Our time cannot be wasted because students' lives are at stake. Planning our time is a habit we must develop through repetition and action. This is why it is so important to set aside weekly planning sessions. Sometimes we spend too much time reacting to the small things that come to our attention, which eat into our daily schedule. You can do two things instead:

- Add it to the *Stomp It Out! Task* list. This way you know you have to do it, but it's not a big priority.
- If you have a time gap, you may want to do the small task immediately to get it out of the way, but add it to your calendar as a record that the task was done. Your absolute mission is to stick to your focus for the day so that you do not get off track.

It takes discipline to keep yourself on track to use your time in effective and productive ways. When working on a larger task, break up the task into bite-size chunks to manage your time wisely. Take each task one bite at a time. Work with the end in mind and build your schedule backward from there. For example, say your principal asks you to conduct a parent training on "How to Help your Child Who Is Struggling Academically." First, you want to know the date of the presentation and how much time you will be given to present. Second, decide what handouts to give to parents and how you will present your talking points through PowerPoint or handouts. Third, plan it on your *Stomp It Out! Tasks*. On your weekly calendar, break the tasks into parts, from working on the presentation to printing handouts. Again, work with the outcome in mind.

The life of a school counselor can be overwhelming at times because so many people depend on you. Know how to say "No" politely or when to close your office door when you are in session with a student or a group of students. So how can you keep from saying "Yes" to everything or everyone?

Start by listening to the request, being polite, and asking questions. This may give time to say, "Here's what I can do for you," and then ask, "Will that work for you?" If you are not sure how to answer, let them know that you will get back to them. And, finally, if you do not have the time in your schedule, let them know that "You are sorry you can't fit it into your schedule this week, but perhaps they can wait until next week." It is important for you to stick to your priorities and not allow others to get you off track. Of course, if your administrator asks you to do an assignment, always ask for the due date. Check your calendar and see whether it can be done during your gap time in the calendar, whether you'll have to rearrange your schedule, or whether you can add it to your *Stomp It Out! Task* as an item to be completed.

If you are in session with a group of students, a parent, or an individual student, always keep a cute sign outside your door that states that you are busy. Here are some of my favorite examples of signs for your office door:

- VIP (Very Important Person) in My Office, please come back.
- Think Tank in Progress, please come back later.
- If the door is closed, please leave me a note.

My own counseling door had a small table outside in the hallway with a notepad, pencil, and a small box with a hole for students to drop me a note when I was not available. My students knew that I was busy either inside or outside of my office. The notepad I made for the students or staff had room for their name, room number, teacher's name, and a place for them to write me a message and drop it in the box. If I was away from my office, I had a spinner hung on my door that stated where I was, such as in a classroom, in the cafeteria, in a meeting, off-campus, etc. Sticking to my schedule was extremely important to me, the staff, the administrators, and the students. They knew exactly where I was. I also posted my weekly/daily schedule outside my office door. Stick to your plan and show off your weekly/daily plan. Others will see how busy you are all day and all week long. You give no room for anyone to say, "What does a counselor do all day?"

Some of us struggle with planning. But if you have no plan, someone else will plan your day for you. For example, say your administrator needs your help to complete a report by the due date of Friday. He notices on your posted calendar that you have open slots all day on Wednesday and Thursday. The administrator assumes that your calendar is clear of activities and now asks you to complete a report that will take two full days. To avoid the assumption that you have free time to spend on non-counseling assignments, start with a thoughtful plan for the week. Your calendar should show a full week of counseling activities, which include individual counseling, small groups, classroom instruction, parent training, staff training, team meetings, school-wide initiatives, and program planning activities. A detailed calendar for the week/day shows the amount of work that must be accomplished, leaving no room for the assumption that you do not have a busy schedule and that you are not serving students.

At the end of the week, you will either have evidence of all the hard work you accomplished or no evidence of your accomplishments. You know you are tired, and that you worked hard the entire week, yet you cannot explain what you completed or what students you met and served. This may be a hint that you lack organizational or time management skills. As Tracey writes, *"Discipline yourself to keep yourself focused on the most valuable use of your time."*[20]

Procrastination is a habit that can keep you from moving ahead mentally and physically. It can cause anxiety, stress, tension, and fatigue. It keeps you from living a happier and healthier life because it always lingers in your head and takes up vital space. It never leaves your thoughts until you decide to change it. You are the only one who can control the day, but if you allow procrastination to dictate your day, it will kill your hopes and dreams. Know yourself and know what needs to be changed. The old cliché says, "Work smarter; not harder." I truly believe in this statement. You will always put in plenty of time, but the time you spend can be done more efficiently if you plan wisely.

Procrastination leaves an elephant in the room that causes a sense of guilt. It can stop you from focusing on your work because you choose to distract yourself or put off a task due to a lack of passion for or understanding of the task. Procrastination is a time robber. Some excuses for procrastination are:

- I am afraid to fail.
- I am afraid of looking stupid.
- I can't do this.
- I would rather sit here and shuffle these papers.
- I should never have volunteered.
- I am too tired to think.
- I hate doing this.
- I am overwhelmed.

So, now what? Procrastination is an all-or-nothing mindset: "What if I mess it up, so I'm not going to start," or, for the perfectionist, "I can't make it perfect, so I'm not finishing it." Both mindsets can impede your work due to your own self-talk and fear. Settle these negative thoughts in your head and start working on the task, one bite at a time. Plan in your calendar. Write the due date in your calendar and work backward by prioritizing each task required to complete the assignment. Spread the task throughout the week or up to the due date. Decide how much of the task you will accomplish today. Continue to push through your plan each day until the job is done. Successful school counselors do what they love, and they get better and better at learning and growing to become extraordinary. These counselors will add purpose to their work by adding value to the hours spent at work versus simply fulfilling the hours required to be at work. Learn to control your time or your day instead of the day controlling you. You can do it!

Be good to yourself and reflect on your successes. Reward yourself for not procrastinating and completing the job on time. Your reward can be simple and inexpensive, like enjoying cake with ice cream, or going to the movies, or any creative ideas you may have. It is important to change a bad habit of procrastination to a more happy and healthy habit that will bring you peace, joy, and happiness. At the end of the chapter, you can view the full version of the School Counselor Time Management System and other time management resources.

Organization

An organized office opens your mind to think creatively and allows distractions to take a back seat. What do you see when you turn on the lights in the morning in your office? If you do not feel good or feel anxious about what you see, then decluttering may need to be where you start to create a less stressful environment. It's not only for you but for your students. A cluttered environment may feel like the walls are closing in. It may cause some anxiety or the feeling of not knowing where to start your day. Clutter can keep you from finding the things that you need to do your work or hinder you from getting to your classroom guidance on time. Your work area should be a stress-free zone where you can work more efficiently and more productively. For example, paperwork will never go away. Paper has no feelings, no tears, no hang-ups, yet school counselors sometimes waste time shuffling through piles of paper just to get their day started. Managing clutter can consume your day.

Everything has a home. It doesn't have to be fancy, just functional. Create a specific place for all items on your desk or in your office, such as curriculum, files, books, office supplies, art supplies, or other such things. At the end of the day, your work area should be organized and ready to go for the next day. This will give you a great sense of accomplishment.

Decluttering Your Space

Let's look at first things first. What's on your desk? Is it functional? Is it cluttered? Take a good look at your desk and visualize it. If you have a stack of papers on your desk, ask the question, "What do I need to do with this sheet of paper?"

- Is it an action item? If so, make a file for it and add it to your *Stomp It Out! Tasks*. Then file it away until needed.
- Is it a completed task? If so, file it away or return it to the owner.
- Is it an information sheet? If so, decide if you need to create a file or toss it.
- Is it something you need? If not, get rid of it.

Do not keep stacks of papers on your desk, moving them from one corner to another. Avoid stacking your papers on top of other things that you may need during the day.

THREE D'S TO DECLUTTERING

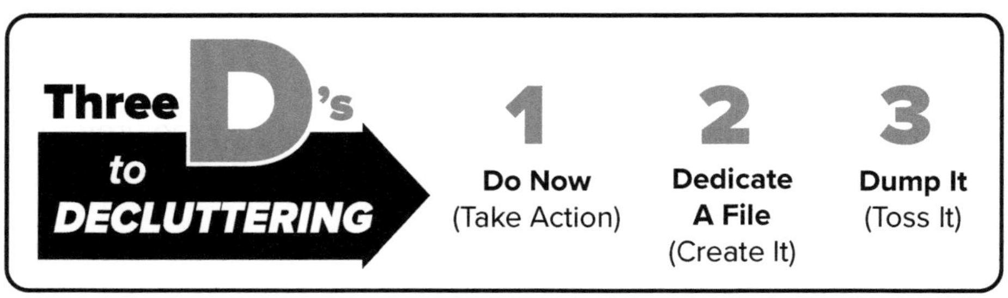

At the end of the year, take the time to purge all unneeded files and prepare for the next school year. For example, you may want to purge old meetings. Don't worry! You will receive other meeting agendas for the upcoming school year to replace what you purged.

Time and organization can be stretched, shortened, and manipulated to meet your goals and complete tasks for the day. Learn to manage time in your own way. As the saying goes, Rome was not built in a day. But we imagine they were laying bricks every hour. Even the busiest of schedules contains "hidden hours" of time. Learn to recognize and find these hours. Keep laying one brick at a time.

THREE D'S TO DECLUTTERING

DO NOW

Take Action:

- Have a due date written in the corner of each action item.
- Add the action item on the *Stomp It Out! Task List*.
- Add to your weekly calendar, giving yourself enough time to do the action item before the due date.

DEDICATE A FILE

Create It:

- Make a file for any information worth keeping for future use.
- Make files according to main topics, such as:
  - Grants;
  - Counselor Meetings;
  - Guidance Curriculum (by grade levels or topics);
  - Career Fair;
  - Resources for Parents, etc.
- At the end of the day, return files to the filing cabinet, to the office, or to the owner.

DUMP IT

Toss Away:

- Try not to spend too much time on items you do not need; toss it away. Get rid of it!
- At the end of the year, purge all your files.

BINDERS

A label maker will help keep your binders looking professional and organized. If you have your label maker handy in your office, it will make life so much easier.

Ideas for Creating Your Binders:

- Purchase a label maker.
- Choose your favorite colors for binders.
- Guidance lessons or small groups—choose colors by lesson topics or by grade levels.
- Return all binders to their original places on the shelf at the end of the day.

TRAVELING COUNSELOR

If you are a counselor who's on the move, carry guidance materials, file folders, and supplies from meetings to classrooms. It is important to always have all your information with you, especially if you do not have time to go back to your office. One suggestion is to purchase a rolling cart that will carry all your supplies and information with you as you travel from place to place. For example, you may have classroom guidance that starts at 9:00 a.m. and immediately afterward you are asked to attend the MTSS meeting at 9:45 a.m. You will not skip a beat because, in your rolling cart, you can carry your guidance materials/supplies, laptop, calendar, notebook, folders, etc., and everything else you need for the meeting and your classroom.

To maximize efficiency and minimize unnecessary effort, consider implementing a structured approach to preparing for the next day. Reviewing your calendar at the end of the day allows you to strategically gather the materials required for upcoming appointments and tasks. Recognizing that our schedules often involve moving between different spaces, a well-organized system for transporting counseling resources is essential. This intentional preparation will save you time, reduce physical strain, and conserve energy, allowing you to focus more fully on your work.

FILING SYSTEM

Did you know that the average person loses an hour a day due to disorganization? Be careful not to fall into that trap. James Young, a systems creator, states, "*What the world does not need is another filing system, but rather a fail-safe retrieval system.*"[21] Whatever system you decide to use, you must adhere to and respect your system. Trust yourself and the system you set up for yourself.

Physical Files

Create a filing system that works for you. Be sure it's done before you leave your office for the day. A good filing system can be paper or electronic. Files should be organized and easy to find. It is important to get a locking file cabinet, especially if you are keeping student files. Decide how you want to organize your filing system based on your "Big Rocks," or big priority items. For example, if you teach a bullying lesson in the month of November, you could organize your lessons by grade level. It is a good idea to keep lessons separated by grade level to meet the developmental needs of your students. Another reason to organize your lessons by grade level is to avoid repeating guidance lessons from year to year, which would be redundant for your students. Guidance lessons should be progressive from one grade level to the next, especially in the elementary years.

It's always a good idea to keep all files in alphabetical order. Prioritize by color, number, letter, or topic, whichever method makes the most sense for you. For example, any lessons created can be filed in a folder by topic and separated by grade level. Separate lessons by grade level so the activities are developmentally appropriate. The important thing to remember is to be consistent—use the system you created and trust it. At the end of the school year, purge old and outdated files. Get ready for the new, upcoming school year.

Your filing cabinet drawers can be labeled as:

- **Action Folder:** Any projects that have an actual deadline. Flagging items with a deadline is another idea for helping you stick to your priorities. Once completed, this folder can go to the back of the drawer with a file labeled "Completed Projects." Keep all projects in alpha order for easy retrieval.
- **School-Wide Projects:** Projects that may repeat year after year (for example: College/Career Fair, Mentoring Program, etc.). Keep files in alpha order.
- **Caseload:** Create folders for students that you frequently work with individually. It is important to keep accurate files on your students.
- **Guidance Lessons:** Folders made for important information, guidance lessons, group lessons, etc. Keep files in alpha order.

Digital Files

In the world of work today, we juggle a million things, including digital files, emails, photos, teleconferences, etc. It can be overwhelming. Time is precious to a school counselor who is juggling 1001 activities all day long. Keeping your sanity while organizing your digital files or searching for a specific email may be chaotic. A digital organization system can be unique for each of us, but it is important to figure out a system that will work for you. You may want to consider some of these suggestions for a digital filing system:

- Delete files that you do not need. Don't try to save everything.
- Just like the filing system using file folders, you can create folders for each of your major file types. Keep each file name short and to the point. For example, you may have a file labeled Guidance Curriculum, and within this file, you may have a separate file per grade level or by topic. Your computer will save your files in alphabetical order, which makes it easier to retrieve your documents.
- Be proactive and be consistent with your digital filing system. And plan for weekly backups to ensure your files are always safe.

Emails

Emails can also be another headache for us. A school counselor may get many emails during the day from the principal, teachers, parents, students, or the community. They also require your time to respond. Below are a few suggestions to keep your sanity intact and keep your inbox clear of clutter:

- Delete, delete, and delete any emails that are not relevant to your job. Do not even open them. For example, advertisements from different companies, voting information, or any other information you deem unnecessary. These types of emails should be deleted first. If you constantly receive unwanted emails, you can always unsubscribe. Keep your inbox clear of clutter. Keep only the emails that you need to respond to or that may require an action step to complete a task.

- Plan an email check-in at least three times a day: first thing in the morning, at lunchtime, and at the end of the day. Be prepared to write in due dates on your *Stomp It Out! Task List*. You may want to print any pages that are action items that may include details and due dates.
- Once you have read an email, do one of two things: delete it or file it in your email file folder. You can create email file folders using a specific name or topic. For example, your principal's emails can be filed under Principal, emails sent from a parent can be filed under Parent, etc. This process should not be complicated.

Managing electronic documents should be part of your overall organizational system. A proper digital system should include all handling of documents, including filing, retrieval, and a clutter-free inbox. Don't give up. Learn to manage your systems well, which will help you manage your time. In summary, planning and organizing are skills that must be developed and formed as a habit.

You may want to take the **Time Survey** and give yourself a rating. There are five common excuses for not planning.

1. I don't have to plan.
2. I already know what I have to do. Why take time to plan?
3. Planning doesn't work for me. I have too many things I need to do.
4. I feel "tied down" when I have a long list of things I need to do.
5. I don't know how to plan properly.

TIME SURVEY

Add a 1, 2, or 3 to each statement below. Count the number of 1s, 2s, and 3s.
Which number has the highest counts?

1 = Room To Improve **2** = Sometimes **3** = Not an issue; I'm good

RATING	
	I use my school time wisely.
	I prioritize my work activities each week.
	I set aside times in the week for counseling activities.
	I schedule some flexible time.
	I use a To Do List.
	I plan with an annual calendar.
	I plan with a weekly calendar.
	I plan a daily calendar with time slots.
	I spend a lot of time reacting to unexpected events.
	I think others control more time than I do.
	Paperwork consumes most of my time.
	Interruptions are common when I am counseling students.
	I prefer spontaneous and unstructured counseling sessions.
	I meet students more in individual than group sessions.
	Most of my counseling with students is crisis counseling.
	I leave every day feeling good about my work.
	There never is enough time in my day to accomplish my goals.
	I often begin the day tired and overwhelmed.
	I am unable to see all the students referred by teachers.
	I am unable to see all the students who refer themselves.
	I am more of an administrative assistant than a counselor.
	I thought I would do more counseling than I am.
	Students think I am doing a good job with my counseling activities.
	Parents appreciate the counseling work that I do for their children.
	I make time to participate in a variety of meetings.

How many did you count in each area? 1s_______ 2s_______ 3s_______

What do I need to do to change the 1s and 2s to 3s? ______________________________

____

What are my strengths (3s)? ______________________________

____

The School Counselor Time Management System

THE DAILY PLAN

Date: ____________________ Circle: MON TUE WED THU FRI SAT SUN

TIME	SCHEDULED ACTIVITY	DONE	NOTES
7:00 a.m.			
8:00			
9:00			
10:00			
11:00			
12:00 p.m.			
1:00			
2:00			
3:00			
4:00			
5:00			

The School Counselor Time Management System

STOMP IT OUT! TASKS

Month of ______________________________

COMPLETED ✔	STOMP IT OUT! (MUST DO)	DUE DATE	PRIORITY STATUS HIGH .... LOW
			1 2 3 4
			1 2 3 4
			1 2 3 4
			1 2 3 4
			1 2 3 4
			1 2 3 4
			1 2 3 4
			1 2 3 4
			1 2 3 4
			1 2 3 4
			1 2 3 4
			1 2 3 4
			1 2 3 4
			1 2 3 4

The School Counselor Time Management System

DAILY & WEEKLY REFLECTIONS

Week of ______________________ **Today's Date** ______________________

REFLECTIONS/NOTES

Connect the Dots to Maximize Student Success

Build bridges not walls

Abhijit Naskar

School counselors are bridge builders. They help lay one brick at a time along a student's path from childhood to adulthood. Counselors support students from entry into Pre-K to exit from high school.

School counselors deliver programs designed to help students develop a strong foundation that leads to long-term success in life and relationships. This foundation is built on Maslow's hierarchy of needs, in which the child's basic needs are met, which makes way for the child's psychological and self-fulfillment needs to be met later in life. The counselor's work is crucial to helping students feel a sense of love, belonging, and belief in themselves. When students' needs are met, they can identify their abilities and function at their highest potential.

MASLOW'S HIERARCHY OF NEEDS

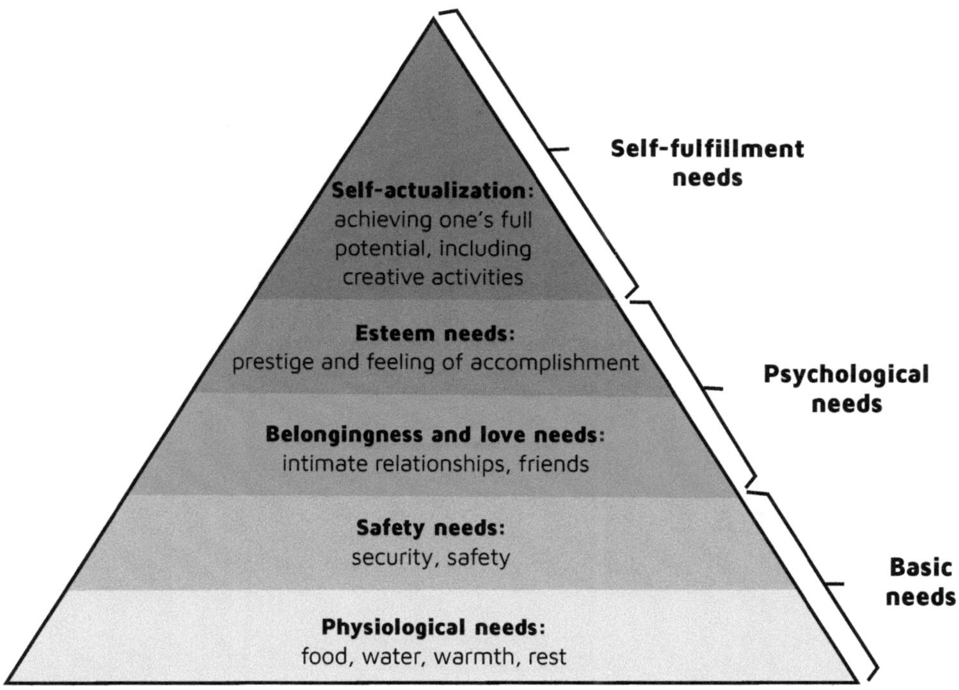

It has been said that "nothing worthwhile is ever easy." In the world of school counseling, this is true. The school counseling program is, by nature, comprehensive and very complex. Advocacy for every child in a school means having a readiness to deal with the academic, personal-social, and emotional needs each student brings to school on a daily basis. But school counselors are not alone in this work. To effectively advocate for students, school counselors must take leadership to engage all stakeholders who have committed to doing their part on behalf of the child. This advocacy takes the form of communication. Communication is the glue that brings stakeholders together to pave the way for students.

The Whole Picture

A school counselor's goal is to ensure that students have the tools they need to be successful in life. The questions we should ask ourselves are:

- How do we know if our students are achieving that success?
- How do we know if we are truly bridging the gap and making a difference for our students?
- How do we know if students are ready and able to connect the dots and become productive citizens in our society?

This concept of "connecting the dots" reminds me of a dot-to-dot picture. In Picture A, we can see the potential of what our students can become. As children, they may not be able to make the connection between where they are and where they will be in the next ten, twenty, or even thirty years. The question for school counselors is how to help students connect the dots and create a whole picture of what success may look like for them, as indicated in Picture B. What can school counselors do to help them see the totality of who they are and what they are able to accomplish in life?

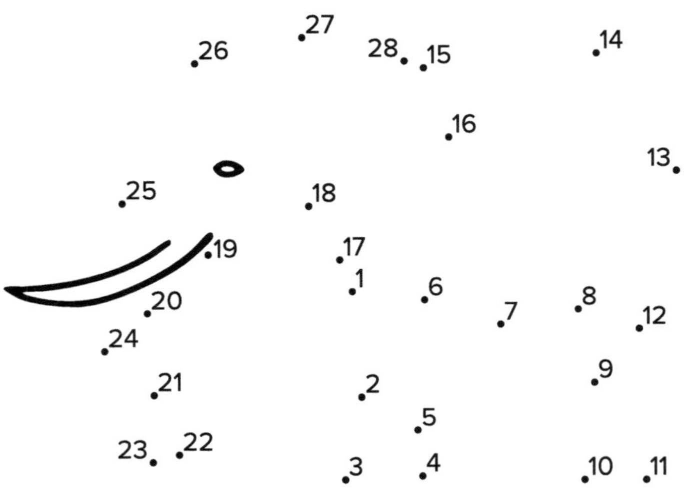

PICTURE A

PICTURE B

To help connect the dots, school counselors must lead the way by engaging in ongoing communication with students and stakeholders. School counselors must master the art of communication and use their programs to let students know what services they provide and how they will deliver those services. School counselors can communicate important information about their school counseling programs through newsletters, websites, school bulletins, school announcements, school profiles, etc.

CONNECTING WITH STUDENTS

Classroom Guidance

One of the great ways counselors connect with students is through classroom guidance. Before I became a high school counselor, I was told that high school counselors have very little time to conduct classroom guidance lessons. I was told that individual planning would consume most of my time and there would be very little time for other activities within the program. As time went along, I realized I was not connecting with my students in a meaningful way. More and more, I felt I did not have a sense of where they were and whether they were moving in positive directions. I began to realize that, if I spent my time in individual planning sessions alone, I would leave out most of my students who needed me just as much.

The art of counseling is the ability to respond to the immediate needs of individual students while at the same time meeting the needs of all students. As a leader of the program, I recognized the importance of a balanced, comprehensive school counseling program. Classroom guidance became a hallmark of success at our high school campus. As a counseling team, we began to leverage our time in classroom guidance to build relationships with our students and answer the broader questions many of them had.

As time went along, my high school students looked forward to us coming to their classrooms (just as much as my elementary students did). Not only did we empower our students to express their thoughts and feelings openly, but we also gave them the confidence they needed to seek help for themselves when they were in crisis. Spending time with our students in a classroom guidance setting was a game changer for them and a welcome activity.

As a school counselor, you may struggle to find time to connect with students in the way you would like. You may have so many demands on your time that you rarely get the opportunity to simply enjoy your time with your students. Classroom guidance is a great way to regain the time you need to help students connect the dots and feel they have an advocate to walk alongside them through their journeys in life.

Topics

The topics you cover in your classroom guidance lessons give students the education and tools they need to address the many challenges they face. You can feel good knowing you are equipping your students with the tools they need to make healthy decisions, build positive relationships, and plan their path to postsecondary study and success.

In the state of Texas, school counselors are responsible for delivering guidance lessons related to the following topics:

Freedom from Bullying
Drug & Alcohol Prevention
Self-Care & Suicide Prevention
Anti-Victimization
College & Career Preparation
Orientation to Counseling Services

As these are certainly topics that are of interest to all counselors, you can check with your state education agency, your county, or your district to find out what topics you should include in your guidance program.

Counseling

Most counselors say the reason they chose to pursue a career in counseling is to help students overcome challenges. Our students suffer from very personal issues, and they need someone to help them make critical decisions. Setting aside time in your schedule to address the immediate needs of your students is vital. There is no better feeling, as a student, than knowing that someone is in your corner, advocating for you. School counselors connect the dots for students when they take time to understand the challenges their students face, problem-solve with them, and connect them to the resources they need to achieve success.

School-wide events

Millard Fuller, co-founder of Habitat for Humanity, is often credited as saying, *"For a community to become whole and healthy, it must be based on people's love and concern for each other."*[22] One of the most important things counselors can do to advocate for students is to help them feel a sense of connection to the school. School-wide events can be a great way to help all students feel good about their ability to learn and achieve. Students feel this motivation when we celebrate them for getting good grades, earning attendance awards, playing sports, and participating in various club organizations. Positive awareness days such as Red Ribbon Week, Social-Emotional Learning (SEL) day, and Random Acts of Kindness week are also great ways to help build a positive sense of community in the school.

School counselors take the lead when they invite all stakeholders to the table to build a strong sense of community within the school. School-wide events help students think positively about their futures. They also give adults the opportunity to work together in the best interest of students.

Connecting with Stakeholders

British writer and lay theologian C.S. Lewis wrote, "*Two heads are better than one, not because either is infallible, but because they are unlikely to go wrong in the same direction.*"[23] When school counselors connect with stakeholders, great things happen for students. Student outcomes improve when we join with parents, teachers, and community members to advocate on behalf of our students.

Teacher Consultation

School counselors connect the dots for students when they collaborate with teachers. School counselors often find themselves educating teachers about the social, emotional, and developmental needs of students. Because teachers interact with students daily, they can speak to students' patterns of behavior in the classroom. However, when problems arise, school counselors can offer their expertise. Because some counselors are teachers first, the classroom experience gives them insight into the teachers' experiences. School counselors who lead great school counseling programs partner with teachers to provide education and information that can help the teachers better serve students. Not only does this give teachers more tools to work with, but it also helps students overcome obstacles in the classroom and paves the way for growth and learning.

How often do you communicate with your teachers? Do they know what services you provide? Do they have a good understanding of the social-emotional needs of their students? Remember, teachers are experts in curriculum and instruction. However, school counselors are experts in human behavior. Communicate often with your teachers and be a resource for them. Indirectly, you will help them and help your students succeed!

The counselor's ability to connect students to professionals who can help fill gaps for them is vital. Counselors must be prepared to respond to students' needs in ways that communicate care and concern for them and their families. Counselors should never feel the pressure to be the "end-all" for students.

Psychotherapist Allison Edwards suggests that "*Counselors are not the strategy for students.*" They *teach* strategies that help students manage their own thoughts, behaviors, and emotions.[24] Counselors connect the dots for students when they assess their needs and effectively connect them with stakeholders who can provide services that fill academic, social, and emotional gaps.

CONNECTING WITH YOUR COUNSELING TEAM

I served in the field of school counseling for twenty-seven years and have concluded that there is no more important asset to building a strong school counseling team than communication. Words and actions help counselors connect. They help counselors come together to plan ways to help students succeed. Oftentimes, before we can get to student success, we must figure out how to find our own success as individual counselors and as counseling teams.

Connecting with your counseling team is key. Weekly team meetings are great ways to connect to discuss and strategize activities pertinent to the success of the school counseling program. Team meetings should occur frequently and should be guided by an agenda.

While working with my lead counselors, it was beneficial to include discussion items that are important to me and allow my team members to add their items for discussion as well. It gives everyone the opportunity to make their voices heard and contributes to the health, growth, and success of the team. When members of the counseling team feel they can make such a contribution, the team wins.

The sample agenda below shows the structure of a district-wide lead counseling team meeting. I allot time for my items and then create a space for lead counselors to add their topics. I create the agenda in Google Docs so that the agenda reflects real-time discussion items. We can also see notes that reflect the items we have talked about, decisions made, and the next steps needed to complete a task.

Lead Counselor Meeting

November 17, 2020 I 9:00 a.m. - 10:00 a.m.

9:00 a.m. Good Things!
9:05 a.m. ParentED - CCMR Sessions
9:10 a.m. Student Attendance Challenges & Considerations
9:15 a.m. District Remediation Plan
9:25 a.m. 2020-2021 Grading Policy
9:30 a.m. Spring Dual Credit Preparation/Training
9:40 a.m. Lead Discussion Items
9:55 a.m. Wrap-up and Close

Lead Discussion Topics:

SCHOOL	TOPIC
MacArthur	REG1212_Emergency Directory

If you are a leader looking for a way to connect with your counseling team members, weekly team meetings are a great place to start. If you have not met frequently, it may be somewhat awkward at first. But if you stay on the course, these moments of connection help build relationships and trust. It is also a good way for team members to better understand each other's idiosyncrasies. The more time school counselors can spend with each other, the greater the opportunities to build trust and camaraderie.

Teamwork can expand your service to students exponentially. Team meetings can be one of the best ways to broaden your capacity because you are building on each other's strengths to act in the best interest of students. In the world of school counseling, it can be a challenge to stop what you are doing to discuss department priorities and plan your school counseling program. The time you pull away to plan your work together is time well spent. Many times, team members can get so involved in the work that they forget to take time to process how well they are delivering the program and whether or not they are serving students in the most efficient ways. Not only that, but if too much time goes by without the team coming together to discuss the work, as with any relationship, you can lose the big vision. I have found that timely, consistent meetings can help everyone stay on track and focused throughout the year.

WEEKLY UPDATE MEETINGS

It was very difficult to stay connected with my elementary, middle, and high school teams during the COVID-19 pandemic in 2020. Because we could no longer meet in person, I felt I needed to ensure consistent "touch base" meetings to clearly communicate district-level processes and procedures. With ninety-six school counselors at thirty-three schools serving more than 33,000 students, weekly update meetings became vital.

Google Docs became our best friend in streamlining information. I created one Google Doc for weekly agendas. I used one slide per meeting to list important discussion topics from one week to the next. Many times, I would invite directors, coordinators, staff from various departments, and community members to present important information to our counseling teams.

As I engaged in conversations throughout the week, I would simply add discussion items and important document links to the running agenda for each level. That enabled everyone involved to keep track of documents that school counselors would need to access later. The running agenda helped us stay organized and eliminated the need to keep up with a multitude of documents.

I embedded the running agenda link in my weekly Outlook calendar invite, which included the Zoom meeting link. This process worked well for school counselors and helped them keep up with all of the information we discussed throughout the year. I am thankful we had digital tools like Google and Zoom to help us stay connected.

Here are samples of the running agendas that outlined our topics from week-to-week. The topics added to the agenda were important reminders that kept counselors on track and focused on priorities. Training, data report reviews, comprehensive school counseling program evaluation, and upcoming events were a few of the topics addressed at each meeting.

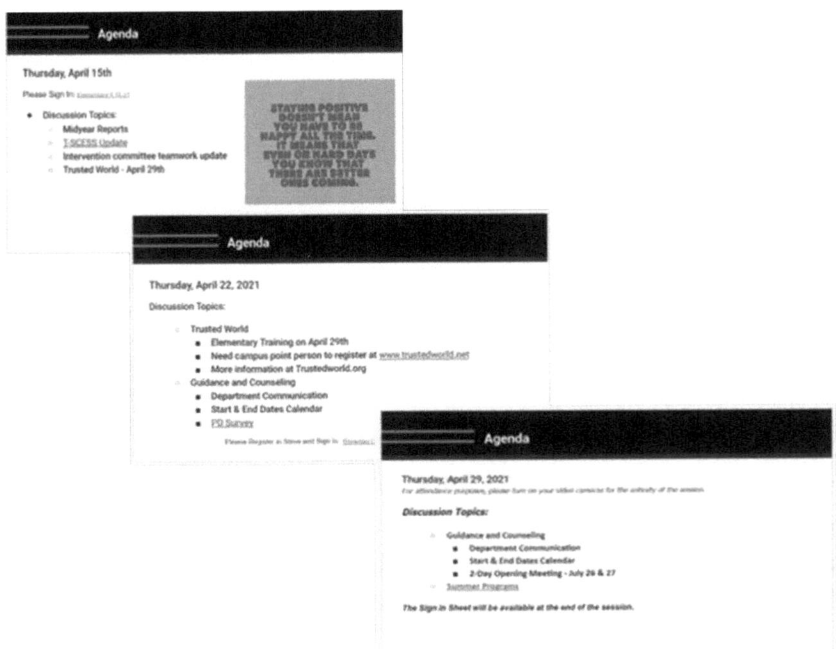

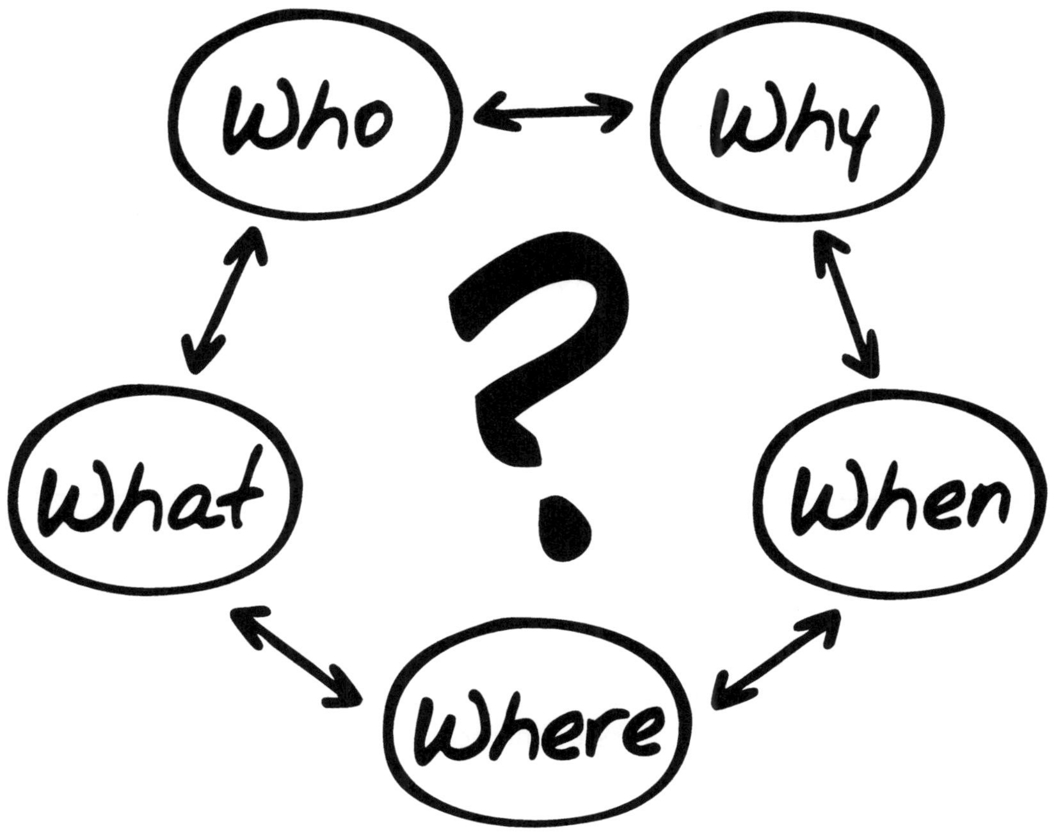

As a school counselor, connecting the dots includes understanding how to organize your work effectively to get positive results for students. Two questions I often get from school counselors are, "How do we know what works for students?" and "How do we know they have achieved success?"

These questions are not easily answered. Because students come with varied needs, we must maintain flexibility in the delivery of school counseling services. We must find a balance between building a structure that guides our service to students and, at the same time, allows time for school counselors to practice that service to proficiency.

As I compose this book, I am also preparing for a meeting to discuss procedures for awarding high school credit to elementary students who complete a dual-language immersion program in elementary school. In one of our weekly update meetings, our school counselors asked about awarding high school credit in middle school. I recognized my counselors needed more in-depth knowledge on how to determine whether students met the criteria for receiving the credit. I began to realize we needed a process to understand the who, what, when, where, why, and how to ensure our students received the benefit of completing their dual-language program and receiving high school credit.

I will use this example as an illustration of how to turn the unknown into opportunities for developing smooth processes that get positive results for students.

WHO?	Elementary students entering middle school.
WHAT?	Award high school credit for dual language immersion program.
HOW?	Follow the steps below: 1. Obtain documentation that helps you identify whether the student has met the criteria for receiving the credit. (Remember to base your decision on documented facts instead of word of mouth). 2. If so, award the credit by completing the Middle School Transcript Audit form. 3. Forward the form to the Data Processing clerk for entry into the student information system. 4. Review the student record to ensure the credit has been awarded.
WHEN?	The awarding of credit should be discussed prior to spring registration to ensure students who should receive the first-level credit do not take the course needlessly. For example: If a student completed the dual language immersion program and earned a credit in Spanish I, the middle school counselors should complete the paperwork to ensure the credit is added to the student record.
WHERE?	Beginning of the middle school year by middle school counselors.
WHY?	The more graduation requirements are met prior to high school, the more time students have to explore other academic options.

When a process is thought through and documented on paper, it makes life so much easier for school counselors. From year to year, you will not have to think and guess your way through tasks because the processes are already in place. Once in place, you can simply tweak and refine them as needed. This allows school counselors more time with their students, as opposed to spending time trying to figure out all the murky details from year to year.

The Whole Child

School counselors must view their programs through the lens of serving the whole child. This is a multifaceted approach that includes many pieces of a larger puzzle. Collaboration is a great way to pull the pieces of your school counseling program together. This job cannot be done alone. It takes teamwork to problem-solve and to implement the school counseling program so that the services provided meet the needs of all students.

Below is an illustration of our interpretation of the many facets that make up the school counseling program, which include the following:

- Vision/Mission
- Leadership
- SMART Goals
- Time Management/Calendar
- Advocacy
- Passion
- Data
- Individual Student Planning
- Guidance Instruction
- Small-Group Instruction
- Action Plan
- Professional Development/Ethics

We must connect the dots with parents, staff, stakeholders, community, etc. to advocate for the student and the school counseling program. Meet *Kaizen*, a Japanese term that sees improvement in productivity as a gradual and methodical process.

The Whole Child: Kaizen

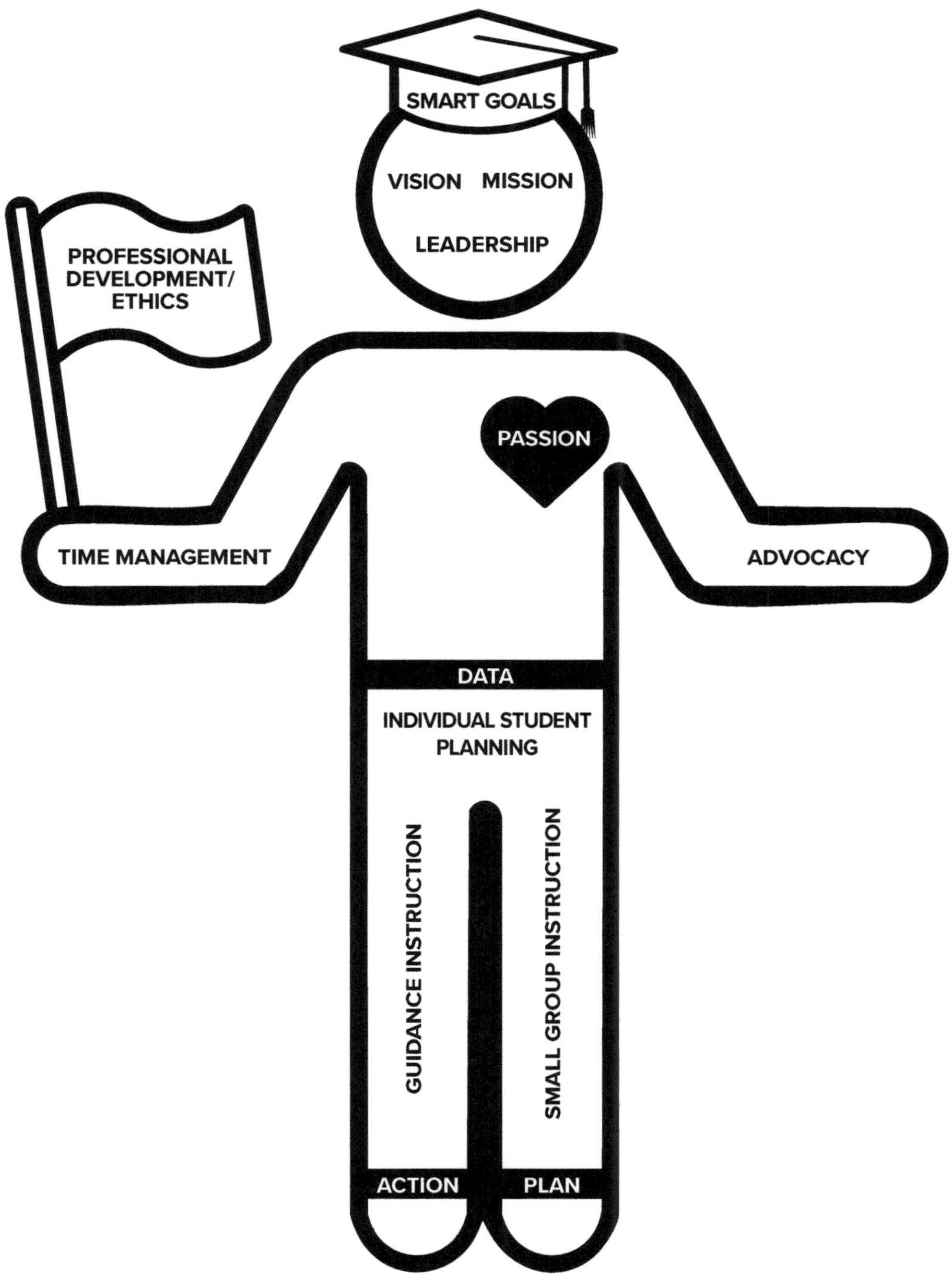

Summary

In this chapter we outlined the critical role of a counselor's intentional approach in identifying and addressing the needs of all students to ensure their success. We have explored how a program design, driven by a vision of success for every student and informed by the intentional analysis of data on achievement, attendance, and discipline, is fundamental to achieving equity and access. Furthermore, the purposeful planning of our annual calendar is essential to protect the time we dedicate to serving students effectively. The chapter also highlighted the vital importance of continuous training and professional development, enabling us to learn and grow in ways that directly benefit our students' needs. In conclusion, our intentionality in both our individual work and the broader school counseling program is the cornerstone of ensuring equity and access for all students, paving the way for their collective success.

CHAPTER 4

BUILDING TO LEAD... LEADING TO BUILD: LEADERSHIP ACADEMY

The love of learning, the sequestered nooks, and all the sweet serenity of books.

Henry Wadsworth Longfellow

The Purpose of Leadership

LEADERSHIP

The role of a school counselor is to promote achievement and social-emotional well-being for all students. To accomplish this task, counselors must be willing to serve as advocates on behalf of their students. Advocacy shows itself in the form of leadership. Counselors must lead their school counseling programs in ways that promote positive, measurable student outcomes. This kind of leadership requires a leadership mindset.

Much of the time, counselors find themselves overwhelmed by the amount of work they are expected to do without ever understanding why they do it. They often find themselves in a cycle of never-ending "to-do's" without taking a step back to evaluate the reason for the tasks. I have found that much of this "busy work" has very little to do with student success. Rather, it is grounded in the work that no one else wants to do, so they "give it to the counselor."

For school counselors to accomplish the overall goals of promoting student achievement and social-emotional wellness, they must see themselves both as leaders on the campus and as leaders of their school counseling programs. Great counselors understand that the only way they can effectively advocate for students is by taking a leadership approach to ensure that student needs are met. Again, this requires a leadership mindset. A leadership mindset takes intentional effort: think like a leader so that you can act like a leader to get things done. Leading an effective school counseling program requires a willingness to grow and develop the organization, maintain effective communication, and develop the implementation skills needed to ensure student success. This kind of leadership is not automatic. It takes intentionality and the willingness to become a great leader of your school counseling program. School counselors can use a leadership academy to become great leaders.

Building Counselor Leaders

In my tenure as a school counselor, I was surprised by the number of people who do not know what school counselors do. They do know counselors do a lot of work, but have a difficult time defining that work. As a counselor who had served at all levels, I consistently asked myself, “How do I know if I am meeting my students’ needs?” I often felt like I did not have a good grasp on measuring the success of my program and therefore was unsure if I was accomplishing the goal.

It wasn’t until I became a lead high school counselor that I began to understand the importance of developing a strong counseling team that worked together to see students succeed. I knew the success of the program would be evident in the success of our students. Building a strong school counseling team requires great leadership that has the heart to see that team succeed. It takes a leader who is willing to learn and grow and help their teammates do the same.

The work of a school counselor is rarely that of a lone ranger. It takes a counselor who recognizes the value of their team and the importance of bringing people together to work on behalf of students. Teams meet the needs of students through constant communication and collaboration between students, staff, parents, and other service providers. Counselors must be willing to lead this collaborative effort to surround students with the support they need to overcome the challenges they face.

In our counseling department, we knew we had great school counselors, but even more so, we wanted to build strong school counseling teams. To accomplish this task, we knew it would require building leadership capacity among all team members. After many conversations in our department, we decided to develop a Leadership Academy for High School Counselors. This decision would eventually lead to the formation of a Leadership Academy for Middle School Counselors and a Leadership Academy for Elementary School Counselors a year later.

The Structure of the Academy

Time is always a factor when it comes to professional development. Counselors have several daily responsibilities on campus that require much of their attention. However, when challenges occur, the counselor’s ability to lead and “take a seat at the big table” plays a huge role in their ability to accomplish program goals. Leadership, for school counselors, is vital to their ability to remove barriers that stand in the way of student success. The time it takes to grow and develop as a leader is worth the investment. It allows counselors to have a voice when it comes to making campus decisions that affect overall student success.

I have found that most counselors want to lead their school counseling programs but may not have the time or the “know-how” to do so. This was the case with many of our lead high school counselors who felt overwhelmed by the vast amount of work required to serve students and lead their teams. Understanding these limitations, our district leadership team decided to extend our normal high school lead counselor meetings by one hour to include leadership development activities, which ultimately became our first Leadership Academy.

AGENDA AND MEETING NORMS

As stated earlier, counselors often have a limited amount of time to engage in meaningful, shared learning experiences. Having an agenda for each meeting will ensure that your leadership academy meeting is intentional and productive. Setting an agenda will build the expectation for the flow of the meeting. It is also vital that everyone come to the table knowing "the rules of the game." Therefore, establishing the expectations ahead of time can keep your meeting positive and focused on leadership development. You can find an example of a leadership academy agenda with meeting norms in this chapter.

The Leadership Academy was devoted to leadership discussions, a book study, campus action plans, and learning logs. In this way, we were able to attend to the practical needs of counselors on the campus, and at the same time engage in leadership training and development.

Leadership Discussions

One of the most important aspects of developing an effective leadership academy is to create a culture where everyone feels heard and appreciated. While every counselor's experience is very different, the ability to speak openly and freely in a nonjudgmental environment is vital to the development of school counselors as leaders. Counselors need to feel that their thoughts and opinions matter. They also need opportunities to hear the ideas of others. When counselors are in the same room together, magical things happen!

The Leadership Academy discussions about the work school counselors do and how they do it become a shared experience. It gives counselors the confidence they need to speak up and speak out to create positive change for students. One of the ways we helped to foster productive discussions in our Leadership Academy was to seek common problems counselors experienced on campus and include them as agenda items for discussion at the next academy meeting. In this way, counselors were able to hear how others were dealing with similar problems and together come up with workable solutions. Leadership discussions can be a great way to help school counselors deal with the many challenges they face when trying to serve their students and work with campus staff.

BOOK STUDY

Book studies can be a great way to help school counselors grow together as leaders. Book studies allow counselors to share ideas that help them improve their understanding of who they are within the context of leading their teams and serving students. The goal of the book study is to foster creative thinking and to explore possible solutions to complex problems.

Materials

Budget is always a factor when it comes to book studies. Because school counselors work with such limited budgets, we decided to set aside district funds to invest in the materials needed for the study. These materials included the book, blank notebooks for notetaking, a binder with binder tabs, and written leadership activities. With the evolution of digital organizational tools, materials needed for your book study can be created electronically. For example, instead of purchasing tangible materials, you can create shared digital folders and subfolders that simulate the physical binder and tabs. Electronic tools like Google Docs, Teams folders, and Live Binders are just a few tools to consider for your book study organization. Concerning the book itself, this can be a topic explored within the development of the book study process. Some participants may want a physical book, and others may be more comfortable with an ebook. To accommodate the learning needs of various team members, you may want to consider the purchase of both.

Book Selection

Early on in the development of the Leadership Academy, our district leadership team engaged high school lead counselors in a discussion about which books they wanted to select for the book study. To save time, we did some legwork beforehand to provide counselors with a list of leadership books with short descriptions. We encouraged counselors to select the book they felt would meet their needs in the area of leadership development. Some of the book titles we explored were books written by authors well-known for their work in leadership development, including Les Brown, John Maxwell, Steven Covey, Brené Brown, Tony Robbins, and many more. Engaging school counselors in the book selection process is important not only to a shared learning experience, but it also helps give school counselors a sense of ownership in the leadership development process.

Pacing the Chapters

After the book is selected, it is important to establish a timeline for completing the book within the school year. Setting realistic goals is important to avoid overwhelming counselors who juggle many responsibilities on campus that require much of their time and attention. The chapters discussed at each session should include relevant activities that are well-planned, focused, and applicable to school counselors' everyday work.

Synergy of Conversation

The success of your book study will depend largely on the organization and structure of the study. However, it will also depend on how free counselors are to share their thoughts about what they learned and what is meaningful to them. When we started our Leadership Academy, we discussed the importance of making sure every counselor felt comfortable sharing their thoughts and ideas in the group.

Meeting norms were created for the book study that included the following 3 P's:

- **Purposeful:** The sole purpose of the book study was for counselors to grow and develop as leaders.
- **Positive:** To avoid the Leadership Academy becoming just another gripe session, we encouraged counselors to maintain a positive attitude. For every problem they brought to the table, they were expected to bring at least two solutions to discuss in the leadership group.
- **Participate:** Counselors were expected to be active participants, which meant they had to read the chapters, take notes, and come back to the group with ideas to share in the next session. In addition, counselors were encouraged to think about the challenges they experienced on campus and apply their new learning from the book study to those particular situations.

Communication

Another goal of the book study was effective communication. During the semester, we discovered that many lead high school counselors were comfortable working with students, but they were uncomfortable communicating with their counseling teams. The book study helped demonstrate the importance of leading and advocating for the school counseling team and the school counseling program. This meant that the school counselor leader was expected to prioritize the goals of the school counseling program to avoid falling into the trap of carrying out non-counseling duties that prevented direct contact with students.

Effective communication skills promote trust and build a sense of confidence and camaraderie. While it is important that school counselors come to the table with their ideas and creativity, it is equally important for counselors to articulate their thoughts and feelings in a way that allows for team planning and mutual understanding of how the school counseling program will look on their campus.

School counseling teams achieve effective communication by meeting initially for annual calendar planning and then on a more consistent basis, either weekly or bi-weekly. Frequent team communication requires skill, patience, and a desire to accomplish the goals of the program together. While school counselors are great at meeting the needs of others, as is the nature of counseling, it is equally vital that school counselors pull aside to take care of their own program needs to allow for effective communication and planning that gets positive results for students. The topic of communication will be discussed in further detail later in the book.

Suggested Activities for Leadership Academy

Below are a few ideas used in the Leadership Academy, which include the following:

- Hedgehog Concept from *Good to Great* by Jim Collins
- Window/Mirror Concept from *Good to Great* by Jim Collins[25]
- Gifts, Talents, and Skills
- Sample Agenda
- Sample Attendance Log
- Homework Assignment
- Learning Log
- Group Projects

HEDGEHOG CONCEPT

Using the idea of the hedgehog concept, school counselors are called to identify how their core values, passion, and motivation impact their school counseling program (SCP) for student success. Each participant received a file folder with three circles, like a Venn diagram. The assignment was to write in the circles: What is your passion as a school counselor? What values do you want to bring to your school and school counseling team? What motivates you to do this job? Afterward, they shared it as a group.[26]

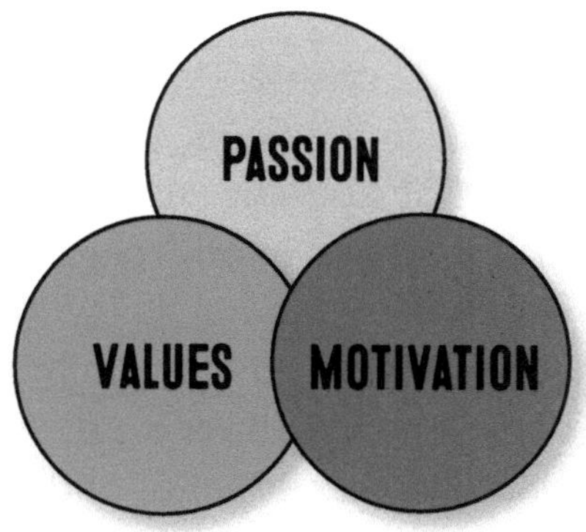

WINDOW/MIRROR CONCEPT

As you prepare to start your Leadership Academy activities, it is important to use activities that drive home the message you are trying to get across to your school counselor leaders. One of the activities we used in our Leadership Academy was the Window and Mirror Concept described in Jim Collins's book, *Good to Great*. Collins uses this concept to teach good leaders how to build credibility with their direct reports and peers by looking outward when giving credit for the team's success, but reflecting inward when things went wrong to see what could have been done to avoid pitfalls. In our leadership academy, it was important to drive this message home with our lead counselors to ensure that they were building a sense of trust with and accountability to the counseling team on their campus. Each participant received a picture of a window looking out to beautiful scenery. Each had to take a moment to look into the picture, think of a time when they were looking outward at a situation, and reflect on how it was handled. Afterward, they shared their experiences with the group.[27]

Leadership is a huge responsibility. The campus looks to the school counselor as a leader who can be a team player and can model vulnerability. Leaders make mistakes. Great leaders reflect on their mistakes and correct them with humility. Great leaders also understand that they do not win by themselves. They acknowledge that it takes dedicated individuals to make a team. When they have created their team, they utilize the strengths of each of their teammates to get things done for students. The window/mirror concept drives home the message that leaders see themselves as a part of the bigger picture, and yet recognize that for every challenge there are lessons to be learned. These lessons create opportunities for growth and a deeper level of understanding about themselves and others. Leaders embrace the common theme that "together we stand and divided we fall."

GIFTS, TALENTS, AND SKILLS

How do you feel when someone gives you a compliment about the great work you are doing? Feels pretty good, huh? Although we serve students because it is in our hearts to do so, it helps our self-esteem when every now and then those gifts are recognized and appreciated. As leaders, we all have the gift to bring out the best in others. Others recognize those gifts and talents through our daily interactions. With the knowledge and skills that we possess, we can create opportunities for others to grow and develop. How? Glad you asked!

School counselors who possess great leadership skills recognize their gifts, talents, and abilities to advocate on behalf of students. Your gift is a call for service to respond to students in need. Your talent, on the other hand, is your unique natural ability. You may have an extraordinary ability to collaborate with others. Therefore, your ability to coordinate a school-wide event to recognize your students who earned perfect attendance may serve as a direct and indirect benefit to students.

School counseling is a gift. It is a call to serve students in need. Your service to students can take many forms (i.e., underprivileged, disabled). Your talents are the unique abilities you bring to the table. Your talents may be seen in your ability to be creative, tech-savvy, or artistic. These abilities are unique to you and can serve as a great benefit to your school counseling program. Your skills are those abilities you have as a result of training and practice. Delivering quality guidance lessons is a skill you can learn and practice. This skill can benefit those students who need to learn valuable life skills that carry on throughout college and in life. When school counselors understand their unique gifts, talents, and skills, they have the confidence they need to take a seat at the table and serve as advocates for students.

What gift, talent, or skill do you possess as a leader? How can you use these characteristics to benefit others? After reading the brief descriptions below, jot down two or three assets you may have in each of these areas. You can also use this activity with your team to help them identify their unique gifts, talents, and skills!

GIFTS, TALENTS, AND SKILLS

Name: ______________________________ Date: ________________

GIFTS A calling, something to be given away in service
I am gifted to...
1.
2.
3.
TALENTS Unusual, natural abilities
I am talented in...
1.
2.
3.
SKILLS Abilities learned through training
I can...
1.
2.
3.

Suggested Books for the Leadership Academy

American School Counselor Association. *ASCA® National Model: A Framework for School Counseling Programs*. Fourth edition. (American School Counselor Association, 2019). www.schoolcounselor.org/ASCANationalModel

Brian Tracy, *Change Your Thinking, Change Your Life* (John Wiley & Sons, 2003).

James Clear, *Atomic Habits: An Easy Way to Build Good Habits & Break Bad Ones* (Penguin Random House, 2018).

Jim Collins, *Good to Great: Why Some Companies Make the Leap from Good to Great...and Others Don't* (HarperCollins, 2001).

Stephen R. Covey, *First Things First* (Simon and Schuster, 1994).

Angela Duckworth, *Grit: The Power of Passion and Perseverance* (Simon & Schuster, 2016).

Carol Dweck, *Mindset: The New Psychology of Success.* (Random House, 2006).

Stuart F. Chen-Hayes, Melissa Ockerman, and McCarty Mason, *101 Solutions for School Counselors and Leaders in Challenging Times* (Corwin, 2014).

Robert Greenleaf, *Servant Leadership: A Journey into the Nature of Legitimate Power and Greatness* (Paulist Press, 2002).

Simon Sinek, *Start with Why: How Great Leaders Inspire Everyone to Take_Action* (Portfolio/Penguin, 2009).

LEADERSHIP ACADEMY

Tuesday, February 21, 2025 • 2:00 – 4:00 p.m.

Administration Building, Room 346

MEETING AGENDA

Sign in

"Good to Great"
Chapter Review

Chapter 5 Discussion
"Hedgehog Concept"

Q & A

NEXT MEETING:

Tuesday, March 28, 2025 at 2:00 p.m. in Room 346

Chapters 6, 7, & 8

LEADERSHIP ACADEMY

HOMEWORK

Name of Book: ______________________________

Author: ______________________________

Read Chapter ____________, pages ______________________________

1. What areas did you identify as strengths?

____

____

____

2. What did you identify as areas for growth?

____

____

____

3. How does what you read apply to your situation?

____

____

____

LEADERSHIP ACADEMY

LEARNING LOG

Team Chair: ____

Date: ____

Members of my team:

Summary of today's book study:

What did I learn from today's book study?

Next Steps:

LEADERSHIP ACADEMY

GROUP PROJECTS

Here are some suggestions for creating opportunities for leadership growth:

- Create district-wide processes for dual-credit process.
- Create a New Counselor Handbook.
- Develop a mentoring program for all first-year counselors.
- Create a Q&A Blog.
- Create PowerPoint presentations for the school board or for your school/community.
- Create Google Doc folder for all the school counselors to access with classroom lessons.

Name one project that you and your team can implement this year:

___

Who will be on your team to help you develop your project?

___

What time and date will you meet?

___

Who will be your targeted audience?

___

Will you be willing to present at a state or national conference or within your district?

___

Summary

School counseling is collaborative and focused on getting positive things done for students. School counselors must understand the role they play in delivering a program that paves the way for students to reach their highest potential. This effort requires school counselors to become effective leaders who understand the purpose of their work and who are willing to speak up on behalf of students.

Leadership Academies can be a great way to accomplish this task. Leadership Academies create opportunities for counselors to engage in meaningful discussions that are collaborative and solution-focused. These discussions are intended and designed to help counselors find various ways to create positive experiences for kids. Book studies can also be a valuable part of the leadership academy. They help to create an in-depth understanding of the need for school counseling teams to work together to promote student success.

I have learned that most counselors want to take their school counseling programs to the next level. However, it requires an intentional focus on learning and growing together as leaders to make this happen. As the saying goes, "You reap what you sow." Implementing a leadership academy in your district can be a truly rewarding experience that helps build a community of hope and trust among school counselors which, in turn, reaps positive results for students. A leadership academy allows counselors to work together to solve problems and address barriers that stand in the way of effective implementation of the school counseling program.

In our district, the first-year implementation of the Leadership Academy for High School Counselors was so successful that our middle and elementary counselors also wanted to be a part of a leadership academy. In response, our team went to work and used the leadership academy model for high school to create leadership academies for middle and elementary counselors. Due to such high interest, we created an application process to select which counselors could take part in the academy at each level. Principal approval was also a vital part of the application process to ensure counselors were able to meet the time commitment of the program. The eagerness of counselors to be involved in building leadership skills at all levels let us know that school counselors wanted to be great leaders for their programs. Our leadership academies helped to equip school counselors with the tools they needed to communicate, collaborate, and implement effective school counseling programs at all levels.

The vision to create a leadership academy can happen with careful thought and intentionality. If you are interested in developing a leadership academy in your district, here are some tips to help you get started!

- Discuss your idea with your counselor leaders or other counselors in your district.
- Think about the timeframe you will need to implement the academy.
- Discuss the structure of the academy and who will be involved.
- Talk about the goals of the academy and how you will measure its outcomes.
- Decide on the number of times you will meet and the activities you will use.
- Plan a budget and decide on the book and materials you will need.
- Decide how you will inform the larger school community of the program's success.
- Celebrate your success.

With careful planning and district support, you too can have an outstanding Leadership Academy!

CHAPTER

5

MAKE YOUR MARK... LEAVE A LEGACY

That is your legacy on this Earth when you leave this Earth: how many hearts you touched.

Patti Davis

The "Ruby Stone" Effect

Think about a ruby for a moment. It's that stunning red stone, admired for its deep color and sheer beauty. Throughout history, rubies have been linked to things like power, wealth, and even royalty. There are some interesting old beliefs about rubies too. One is that they can really get you going, helping you find the energy to set and reach your goals. Another, more emotional idea, is that rubies represent love, passion, energy, and strength. It's seen as a stone that gives the wearer courage–that extra bit of bravery to face whatever life throws their way.

This idea of the "ruby effect" hits home when we think about what it means to be a school counselor. We're often the heart of the school–the compassionate ones, the ones with a real fire in our bellies when it comes to standing up for our students. We're definitely more than just teachers; we're trained professionals with master's degrees and advanced certifications, specifically here to support students and their emotional well-being. But let's be honest, we're human too, and sometimes our emotional reserves get low. That's when that negative self-talk can creep in and drain us.

We all have those moments when it feels like a dark cloud just won't lift. You might even find yourself thinking things like, "I just can't do this anymore," or, "I'm completely overwhelmed," or, "Nobody gets how much I'm juggling." That's a signal that we need to give ourselves a break–even just ten minutes to quiet all those voices in our heads. Maybe that's a few minutes of peace in your office, a quick walk around the building, or even just a short trip out to your car and back. The truth is, we can't be our best for our students and colleagues if we're not taking care of ourselves first.

Think RUBY

R	**Reflect intentionally:** Carve out moments to consider your priorities, set realistic intentions for the day, and identify what can be released or delegated.
U	**Understand your capacity:** Acknowledge that you are a dedicated professional, not a superhero. Recognize your limitations and proactively seek the necessary supports and systems to sustain your well-being and effectiveness in your purpose.
B	**Build resilience through self-care:** Prioritize practices that nurture your emotional, physical, and mental well-being as foundations for navigating the inherent challenges of the profession.
Y	**Your impact is significant:** Remember the profound difference you make in the lives of students and within the school community. Your dedicated work truly matters.

Here are my affirmations: I'm courageous. I'm strong. I'm fearless. I'm kind.

What are some personal affirmations you can use?

____

____

P.A.T. Yourself on the Back

In my work with school counselors, I have found that many, if not all, are extremely dedicated to their work. They go above and beyond expectations and are always looking to get it done for students. But every now and then, school counselors need to take the time to P.A.T. themselves on the back. What does this mean?

P.A.T. stands for:

- **P**lan
- **A**ct
- **T**ake a Break

The coauthor of this book, Dr. Sylvia Lopez, was an amazing mentor to me when I was a high school counselor. When she began her journey as the Director of Counseling Services, she challenged us to implement a balanced, comprehensive school counseling program that meets the needs of all students. I must admit (and I think many school counselors at that time would agree) that we really didn't have a program before she came to our district. Dr. Lopez challenged us to plan our work, implement our plan, and then take a moment to reflect and celebrate our successes.

Now that I have the awesome privilege of sitting in Dr. Lopez's seat, I often find myself encouraging our school counselors to P.A.T. themselves on the back. I find that counselors are often stressed because they truly do not have a plan for success. They are working hard, but they have no roadmap to measure how well they are doing to help students reach their goals. Without a measure, it is hard to know when you have reached your goal. Those counselors who can measure their success should stop, reflect, and celebrate that success. When school counselors take time to P.A.T. themselves on the back, not only is it a feel-good moment professionally, but it is a personal win to know that you are truly making a difference.

I recall a conversation I had with a school counselor who was extremely overwhelmed with all of the daunting tasks she had to do. Her campus had a vacancy, and she was the only counselor serving the entire student body. In my talk with her, she revealed that she was exhausted, stressed, and about to throw in the towel. She felt underappreciated and did not see the value in doing anything but getting the job done. Suddenly, I realized this counselor needed a P.A.T. on the back. She needed a clear plan of action to guide her throughout the day, she needed time to carry out her plan, and she needed time to pull away to simply enjoy her work with her students. I must admit, she was very hesitant when I encouraged her to step away from her desk and go out into the halls to talk with her students.

All too often, we get caught up in the minutia of paperwork, scheduling, and data entry. So much so that we forget the joy that comes with interacting with our students to help them feel good about themselves and what they can achieve. The enormous amount of work needed to help them succeed often makes us feel bogged down and discouraged. We lose hope. We forget that our purpose as school counselors is to lift up our students and encourage them to keep going. The only way we can do this is to seek encouragement for ourselves and feel good about our ability to make a difference. The only way we can make a difference for others is to experience encouragement for ourselves.

Whenever you are feeling exhausted, frustrated, and ready to throw in the towel, I want to encourage you to P.A.T. yourself on the back. Approach your day with a clear plan of action, be intentional about implementing your plan, and take a break. Every now and then, take some time to step away from your desk, leave the paperwork behind, go out into the hallways, and connect with your students. Allow yourself to experience their world. Allow them to see that you are open, available, and eager to be in their presence. This kind of interaction goes a long way. Many students would not otherwise come to your office to have a conversation. By pulling away from your office, you give them access to the benefits that come from your positivity, encouragement, love, and service. Do yourself a favor: plan your work, work your plan, and give yourself the gift of time! Take some time to P.A.T. yourself on the back!

Personality Challenges

As a director or school counseling team leader, another challenge you may face when working with colleagues or staff is that they can empty your emotional tank. There are several challenging personalities that I have worked with in different school situations. These challenges can be seen in several ways.

The first challenge comes from the "TTWWADI" group (pronounced as *ta-wah-de*), which means *that's the way we've always done it*. The educators who suffer from TTWWADI are some of the most challenging to work with when introducing a new idea or simply changing ways of doing a certain task year after year. This can also be called a *"fixed mindset."* Those with a fixed mindset are unwilling to learn new and different ways of completing tasks. Some of our very own school counselors are set in their own ways and do not want to change. They want to keep doing the same thing repeatedly. In other words, they are happy being in their comfort zone.

The second most challenging attitude is the *"victim mentality."* It's a *"poor little ol' me"* attitude. Some may say things, such as:

- No one understands my job, poor little ol' me.
- I'm too busy to do groups, poor little ol' me.
- I can't talk to my principal, poor little ol' me.
- I have too much to do, poor little ol' me.
- I do everything by myself, poor little ol' me.

Teach yourself or others to go from *Poor Little Ol' Me to Change Your Thinking and Do Something.*

"Poor Little Ol' Me" Thinking	"I Will" Thinking
No one understands my job.	Train my staff about my role as a school counselor and market myself.
I'm too busy to do groups.	Learn to plan my month, week, and day. Stick to my plan.
I can't talk to my principal.	Make an appointment and review my Annual Administrative Conference with my principal.
I have too much to do.	Learn to get organized and celebrate my successes.
I do everything by myself.	Get involved and invite staff to be part of my advisory council or form working teams. I will ask for help when needed.

While it's understandable to feel disheartened by school challenges, a sense of shared responsibility for creating a positive environment is crucial. School counselors who are dissatisfied have the potential to be catalysts for change by exploring new approaches and adjusting their perspective. Think of the "Ruby Effect" and rehearse your affirmation or give yourself a P.A.T on the back.Ultimately, a positive school climate is the result of each individual's commitment to fostering a more constructive mindset.

I can guarantee you that if you help your colleagues or others think differently by changing their attitudes and doing something positive, things will start to look different. Teach adults and students to be thankful and remind them that they are sitting in that very important role in their life's journey. Author and motivator Karen Kaiser Clark wrote a book entitled *Life is Change, Growth is Optional.*[28] It is up to us to choose wisely.

BEHAVIORS

Below are some of my favorite characters. Can you identify yourself or your coworker? Is there a picture that best describes you? Do you exhibit more than one behavior in different situations?

The Golden Retriever Group

Big heart, loves people, sensitive to the needs of others, doesn't want to rock the boat, and doesn't stick to tasks very well.

The Eagle Group

Leads the group, sees the task at hand, is laser-focused on the task, pushes through tough assignments, never makes excuses.

The Sloth Group

Slower pace, prioritizes minimum effort, may lack clear direction, hands-off approach.

The Ant Group

The "worker bees"—know how to collaborate, do not need a lot of prompting — get the job done, reliable.

NAME YOUR BEHAVIOR

What personality matches you?	Description	How do you rate your personality? 1 (not me)– 5 (definitely me)	Why did you select this personality?
	Big heart, loves people, sensitive to the needs of others, doesn't want to rock the boat, and doesn't stick to tasks very well.		
	Leads the group, sees the task at hand, is laser-focused on the task, pushes through tough assignments, never makes excuses.		
	Slower pace, prioritizes minimum effort, may lack clear direction, hands-off approach.		
	The "worker bees." Know how to collaborate, do not need a lot of prompting—get the job done, reliable).		

END OF THE YEAR REFLECTIONS

Date: ___________________________

What did you learn this year as a school counselor?

___

___

___

I wonder...

___

___

___

What areas do I need/want to improve for the next school year?

___

___

___

What will I do differently next year?

___

___

___

How will I get it done?

___

___

___

In a perfect school counseling world, I would....

___

___

___

MY DAILY GRATITUDE JOURNAL

MORNING

THREE THINGS THAT I AM GRATEFUL FOR:

1. ______________________________
____

2. ______________________________
____

3. ______________________________
____

THREE THINGS THAT I WILL ACCOMPLISH TODAY:

1. ______________________________
____

2. ______________________________
____

3. ______________________________
____

EVENING

BEST PART OF MY DAY

(CHOOSE A MOMENT THAT MADE YOU LAUGH OR BROUGHT JOY):

____

____

____

____

Take a Risk

A growth-mindset school counselor will take risks and try new things. The definition of a risk-taker is someone willing to accept new ideas and apply the new learning to benefit the students and the school counseling program. These school counselors are curious and love to learn. If a strategy does not come out as planned, a growth-mindset counselor will see the problem as a learning opportunity and will not be afraid to try again. This is one ingredient to greatness, which is a "never give up" attitude. They will take a chance on something that sparks emotion in their newfound learning. They have a sense of adventure and a willingness to chart a new path. You will never hear a risk-taker say, "That's not my job." Every opportunity is an adventure.

A school counselor who is a risk-taker or has a growth mindset enjoys tackling difficult tasks, solving problems, and seeking feedback from others. A counselor with a growth mindset treats the job like a giant puzzle broken into 1,000 pieces, putting one piece at a time together to form the bigger picture. Most people will take the path of least resistance and default to their comfort zones. A risk-taker will step out courageously, which means that you may have to take a risk when you advocate for your school counseling program. You may have to step out of your comfort zone and teach other educators about your program. A risk-taker or growth-mindset counselor models courage, grit, perseverance, and passion.

A short story by writer Mort Laitner follows a character named Arlene. Arlene is an elderly person who lives life to its fullest, takes many risks, and has no regrets. This is how she sums up her feelings on risk:

> *Here's why I take risks: because I don't want to end up in a nursing home or in a pine box with the I-wish-I-had-done-that look stuck on my mouth. When I walk into an old age home and look at those "senior citizens" I see faces scrunched up as if a lemon wedge was sutured to their lips. Those folks took few risks. They led a safe bitter life filled with fear and hesitation. They squandered life's opportunities. There are no second chances.*[29]

This is a great illustration of being a risk-taker. You will either be content and live in a comfort zone or be adventurous and live life to its fullest. Embrace change and take the journey.

COMPETENT LEADERSHIP

When leading school counselors as a director or as a lead counselor, it can be challenging to get everyone on board and moving in the same direction. The challenge is working with so many personalities and attitudes at once. It takes time to learn who your counselors are, what makes them tick, and what makes them excited to learn. For your school counselors to grow, sometimes they may have to learn a new way of doing things, unlearn the old ways, and relearn how to apply the new ways of thinking. This takes practice and patience. Some school counselors may suffer from growing pains. But that's okay. Once they have learned it and pushed through it, they will move in the same direction.

One piece of advice I learned as a Director of Counseling Services is to "Do what I can with what I have, from where I am." It takes time to grow your team of school counselors.

The most important thing is not to lose faith in them.

We are all like guppies swimming in many different directions until you can lay out the vision, mission, purpose, and direction of the school counseling program. Things may look chaotic. Soon, all the little guppies will be swimming in one direction. It takes your competent leadership to teach, demonstrate, visit their schools, provide positive feedback whenever possible, and have courageous conversations with others.

If you have their best interest at heart, most school counselors will do anything to be the best, because they know there is someone working on their behalf. Dedicated and outstanding school counselors will do what it takes to serve all students.

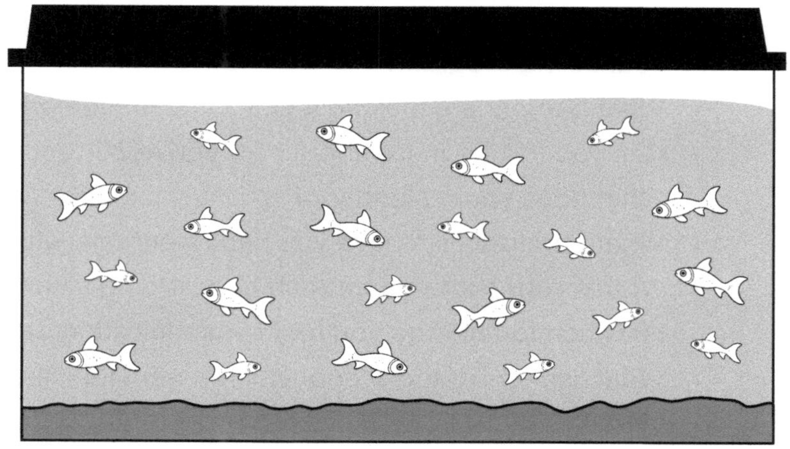

HELPING EMPLOYEES GROW

If you are a director and responsible for school counselors, you must be willing and ready to advocate, train, take risks, and do what's best for all your school counselors. James Clear writes, *"...perseverance, grit, and willpower are essentials to success, but the way to improve these qualities is not wishing you were a more disciplined person, but by creating a more disciplined environment."*[30] I hate to admit it, but sometimes directors get caught up in not fulfilling their potential. Clear describes it this way: "*You don't have to be the victim of your environment; you can also be the architect of it.*"[31]

Let us not forget that being a director responsible for school counselors and a school counseling program is more work than most can imagine. It's bigger than you. If done correctly, there should be no question as to your responsibilities in the school district. Directors are not hired to please everyone but to make critical decisions that impact all school counselors within their districts. Positive or negative, that impact filters all the way down to the schools, staff, and finally to the students. There is no time to waste. As directors, we must commit to the laser-focused work at hand. At the same time, be open-minded, collaborative, and work with the end in mind.

As a director, I always knew that I must help the team grow or go. You learn which school counselors can do the job well and who may need additional help. However, the only way to know which ones are up to the job is by visiting their school campuses and talking to the administrators in charge. I was fortunate enough to visit many of my school counselors when they were teaching instructional/guidance lessons in the classroom or working on special events. School counselors were amazed and excited to see that I took the time to stop by to see them. Counselors who are doing a terrific job at their schools cannot stop talking about all the wonderful things they are doing with their students. They want you to see all the great work displayed on the school walls, created by the students. The principals will tell you they have the best school counselor in the world. I always left these campuses knowing that their counselors had it all together.

Unfortunately, there were also times when I had to visit a campus with a struggling school counselor. My first visit was to have a conference with the principal and to hear about the issue from the principal's point of view. Then I would visit the school counselor to hear their side of the story. As you know, there are always two sides to a story. These conversations are difficult. Sometimes, it was a personality clash between the principal and the school counselor. Or the school counselor was feeling a sense of burnout due to working with no administrator's support or struggled with family issues. Whatever the situation, as a director, you must be ready to deal with any situation. You can either help struggling counselors grow, find mentors for them, or replace them.

It's important to ask questions and, when appropriate, ask for documentation. I based all of my questions on what I learned from the principal's conversation, or I had my own starter questions. Here are a few of the starter questions I had ready to facilitate an open and honest conversation with the school counselor:

- What are some of the biggest challenges you're currently experiencing with your school counseling program?
- What barriers are making it difficult to implement your school counseling program effectively?
- Can you tell me more about how you're currently managing your school counseling program?
- What does your calendar of activities look like right now?
- What opportunities have you had to engage with students in the classroom recently?
- What's your current approach to providing small-group counseling?
- How comfortable do you feel communicating openly with your principal about your program?
- What aspects of the school environment feel like a good fit for you, and what might make it an even better fit?
- Have you considered whether a different school level might better align with your strengths and interests? If so, what positive changes would come as a result?
- What kind of support would be most helpful for you in moving your program forward?
- Are there any specific training opportunities that you feel would benefit your work and the program?
- What steps could we explore that might contribute to your overall professional satisfaction here?

These are crucial conversations. It's important to establish trust with your school counselors to enable such open and honest communication. Not all school counselors are meant to be school counselors. It is hard work. However, it is not all about the work per se, but about the heart of the counselor. I have always believed that you cannot teach a person to have a heart for students. That quality is innate; either they have it or not. If they have the heart, then we can teach them how to become an outstanding school counselor. Both directors and counselors must keep in mind that the number one priority is always the students they serve.

PROFESSIONAL GROWTH PLAN

A Professional Growth Plan (PGP) is not necessarily a negative plan. It is really there to help guide the employee to have a successful learning year. As a director, it is your responsibility to help any counselors who may have derailed get back on track. It is normal for some of our employees to stray, but they must know that you have their backs and are willing to assist and guide them. This takes time and a great deal of energy to implement, but at the same time, it builds trust among your team members.

I believe that working with students is sometimes easier than working with some adults. The different personalities and attitudes of adults, all living under the same schoolhouse roof, can be very time-consuming and challenging. James Clear says it best: "*What's the cost of doing a poor job? What's the cost of doing a mediocre job? What's the cost of doing an exceptional job? Which price are you willing to pay?*"[32] The cost of poor or mediocre employees is our reputation as school counselors and, most importantly, the failure to serve our students with integrity. It's important to remember that a school counseling department or a team of school counselors is only as good as its weakest link. As leaders, we are responsible for doing the work of helping our school counselors grow and be the best they can be.

LEARN TO DELEGATE

An important job of a director is to understand the role of delegating. In order to delegate, you must be willing to trust others to help you carry your vision with integrity. Delegating is part of how you develop and train your school counselors. You can quickly assess who can step up to the plate, work as a team, stay positive, and be willing to do quality work. You may be the only director in your district, or you may have coordinators working on your counseling team. Whatever the situation, you must learn to trust your employees and allow them to take on the leadership role.

FOLLOW-UP AND FEEDBACK

It's important to have a follow-up conversation in writing to record the highlights of the visit with your school counselor and the administrator. In your feedback, you may want to include some celebration of their work, a summary of the challenges they face, and always end with more positive remarks. For each challenge mentioned, include a solution based on the decisions made by the school counselor or the administrator. You can create this document in a variety of ways, such as a Google form, an email, or a letter. Whatever method you use, it is a record of the conversation, held on a specific day and time, that outlines the priorities and ways to improve the school counseling program in that specific school. In addition, documentation is critical to have for any unforeseen situations. Keep a journal for each day, keep it current, and keep it confidential.

COUNSELOR-IN-ACTION: GUIDANCE OBSERVATION FORM

School Counselor: ______________________________ Date: ____________________

Visited by: ____________________________________ Title: ____________________

1. What were the students doing in the class?

2. What were the objectives of the lesson presented?

3. What activities/strategies did the counselor implement during the lesson to reach the objective?

4. What materials/resources did the counselor use during the lesson?

5. How did the school counselor assess students to see if the objectives of the lesson were successful?

______________________________________ ____________________

Signature Date

Role: ______________________________________

Comments/Feedback: ____

____

____

Make it Count!

> *If you are going to live, leave a legacy. Make a mark on the world that can't be erased.*
>
> **Maya Angelou**

WHAT LEGACY WILL YOU LEAVE?

Your life matters. The choices that you make will become part of the legacy you leave behind. The quality of life that you choose by learning, creating, serving, and being your best self will definitely leave a footprint on your legacy. If you have a big dream, go for it. If you fail at it, it's okay. It just means that you are one step closer to that dream. Dreams require effort, and dreams without goals are only dreams. Take your chance and dream big. We have only a short time on this earth. Make it count.

Motivational Speaker Les Brown provides a great illustration of a dream that never developed and subsequently died. He relates:

> *Imagine being on your deathbed, standing around your bed, the ghosts of the ideas, the dreams, the abilities, the talents given to you by life. But, for whatever reason, you never acted on those ideas, you never pursued that dream, you never used your talents, we never saw that leadership, you never used your voice, you never wrote that book, and they are standing around your bed, looking at you with large, angry eyes. "We came to you and only you could have given us life. Now, we must die with you, forever." The question is, if you die today, what ideas, what dreams, what abilities, what talents, what gifts will die with you?* [33]

Think about it. This is your life. What you decide to do or not do is totally up to you. Make your life matter. Don't just exist in this life, live with passion and vigor. Go big and dream big. Imagine the life you want to live. Do what you love to do. Be fearless and live each day as if it were your last. This is your moment; make it count.

Activate your actions as a school counselor. There are only a few hours each day to communicate with your students. You may be the only counselor that a student can connect with during the day or the only counselor that will make a difference in that student's life. Your students are your number one priority. All other things in the counseling world are secondary. Students may not remember what they learned in ninth grade or any grade, but they will certainly remember how you made them feel. The impact you have on students on any given day may speak volumes about your legacy.

LEADING WITH HEART (PASSION)

> *Love is rooted deep in strength.*
>
> **Unknown**

The world around us never stops. The sun will rise, and the sun will set each day, but it's how we fill our day that matters. Do we make the day work for us, or are we miserable in our work or life? This day, and all the other days, are up to us to make worthwhile and full of joy. We have a choice, but sometimes we get lost in the mundane things of life, which makes it very difficult to see the light at the end of the tunnel. You must learn to stop, breathe, and stand still for a second. Don't let the little things pollute your day. This can cause you to lose your focus and your passion. This brings me to a poem called *Lost*.

Lost

by David Wagoner

Stand still. The trees ahead and bushes beside you
Are not lost. Wherever you are is called Here,
And you must treat it as a powerful stranger,
Must ask permission to know it and be known.
The forest breathes. Listen. It answers,
I have made this place around you.
If you leave it, you may come back again, saying Here.
No two trees are the same to Raven.
No two branches are the same to Wren.
If what a tree or a bush does is lost on you,
You are surely lost. Stand still. The forest knows
Where you are. You must let it find you.[34]

It is true we must stop and stand still. Live in the present, in the here and now. Hold strong to your belief and find your heart and soul. Listen to your heart and know where "here" is and be a service to others. We, as counselors, must do all we can to help students who are struggling and hurting. We must guide and teach our students how to deal with life's challenges and provide the tools to help them through any crisis.

Robert Greenleaf, in his famous book *Servant Leadership,* writes that "*the servant leader is servant first.*"[35] Greenleaf describes many characteristics of a servant leader, but one of the most important characteristics is a desire to serve. Other important characteristics include listening, understanding, acceptance, and empathy. This is "you" and the world of school counseling. You are a servant first when it comes to helping your students, families, or coworkers.

As long as I can remember, I've truly believed that *if a student's heart is hurting, the brain stops thinking*. As a school counselor, I led with my heart first, then my head, into decisions that involved a student struggling with their emotions. Many of our students are hurting for many reasons, whether it's a breakup, neglect, or abuse. Whatever the reason, we must seek to understand and feel for the child whose heart is broken inside. We must be ready to guide this child through a dark period of their life and give them a sign of hope. School counselors can change and make a difference in a student's life. You may not see the full benefits of your work right away, but it is that seed of hope that school counselors instill in their students. Ten years from now, a student may not remember what they learned in 7th grade or any grade, but they will remember how you made them feel.

There is a reason why school counselors are known as the "heart of the school." Great counselors know their students, their families, and their struggles, inside and out. Plato says, "*The part can never be well unless the whole is well.*"[36] That's our job. We work with the whole child, not just part of them.

TAKING CARE OF YOURSELF

Do you feel that sometimes your life or your day is spiraling out of control? And you feel like you are looking down at a deep, dark well, falling deeper and deeper inside? How do you make it stop? What if your heart and mind are not right? How do you find passion when you do not have joy in your heart? Some counselors may feel a sense of "I don't care." "I'm tired of dealing with so much hurt." "I just want to quit." Have you ever felt that way?

If that's you. Stop, take a breath, and live in the moment. Don't unpack and live in that dark and negative well of your mind. The only control you have is to change your thoughts and change your thinking. We are all humans, and we all have our moments.

It's time to get a "checkup from the neck up." Change your thinking by getting rid of those pesky thoughts that make you angry, hurt, or unhappy. Brian Tracy writes, "*A negative emotion exists only because we give them life and keep them alive. A stronger emotion will dominate and override a weaker emotion, and whichever emotion you concentrate on grows and becomes stronger.*"[37] It's time to let it go, give yourself a pass, and find the joy in your work, in others, and in yourself. The sooner you can get out of your stinking thinking; the sooner you can refocus, reflect, and give yourself time to find the joy in your heart. Joy is an emotion that makes life, work, and family worth living for in the moment. Joy is deep in the core of our passion.

The best career advice I have ever heard went something like this:

Don't attach yourself to a person, a place, a school district, or a project. Attach yourself to a mission, a calling, or a purpose. That's how you keep your power of positive thoughts, peace, joy, kindness, happiness, and hope.

Seek what makes you happy and what brings joy to your heart. There is a flame of HOPE in your heart. You can begin filling your heart with hope by practicing the following:

- Count your blessings.
- Let go of what you cannot control.
- Practice kindness.
- Listen to your heart.
- Be thankful.
- Just breathe.

What is your passion? Is it writing, singing, creating, living life to its fullest, or being a school counselor? If you can name your passion, congratulations. If you cannot name your passion, it's never too late to search for it. Passion is your vision with action.

Struggles that may come our way are opportunities for us to learn and grow from experience. It may overwhelm us at times, but that's even more reason to stop, breathe, and live in the moment. Brian Tracy says, "*...if you look upon every step forward as a learning experience and every setback as a valuable lesson that has been sent to you to make you stronger and better, you will not be afraid to launch in faith into the unknown.*"[38] We all have a choice to think negative or positive thoughts. Focus on what's important.

Life is a journey, but it is how we handle this journey that makes the difference. Dark chapters in our lives are not the end. Tough times can take you down or push you forward. When you shift your thinking to the lesson to be learned, you plant that seed of greatness, nourish it with positive thoughts, and grow to assume the best. We are school counselors to help spread hope, peace, kindness, and love.

IGNITE THE FLAME OF HOPE

You are the heart of the school and the flame of hope. You do what is right on behalf of your students. You teach them well and continue to plant the seeds of hope. All students must be taught joy, peace, patience, kindness, goodness, gentleness, faithfulness, and self-control. But it must be modeled first. Students learn best by seeing what is modeled before them. If parents are not modeling these behaviors, it is up to us to show them. All students deserve the best of hope. It is our responsibility to help all students, not just a few. Sometimes our wells are dark and deep, but school counselors need to reach in to help heal, encourage, and be that gift of hope to someone else. You can't change everything, but you can change some things. A famous aphorism states, *"Yesterday is history, tomorrow is a mystery but today is a gift. That is why it is called the present."* Live in the moment, be courageous, and embrace your responsibility with joy.

A husband who lost his wife to the horrific national tragedy of September 11, 2001, found one of her notebooks under the seat of the car, and it read:

We have only a finite number of days on earth,
make each day extraordinary and
fill them with passion.[39]

Leave a footprint of hope as a school counselor. Fill your day with love and joy, and make a difference in someone's life!

DOWNLOADABLE RESOURCES

THE RESOURCES IN THIS BOOK ARE AVAILABLE FOR YOU AS A DIGITAL DOWNLOAD!

Please visit **ncyi.org/downloadable-resources** to access the downloadable resources.

Enter the code below to unlock the resources:

LEADER589

To find the latest version of the ASCA® worksheets visit:

https://www.schoolcounselor.org/Recognition/RAMP/Templates.

- Advisory Council Agenda
- Advisory Council Minutes
- Annual Administrative Conference
- Annual Calendar
- Classroom and Group Mindsets and Behaviors Action Plan
- Closing-the-Gap Action Plan
- Lesson Plan

NOTES

1 Angela Duckworth, *Grit: The Power of Passion and Perseverance*. First Scribner hardcover edition. (Scribner, 2016).

2 Duckworth, Grit, 149.

3 Mary Kay Ash, *Mary Kay on People Management* (Warner, 2009), 98.

4 Carla Hayden, "Remembering John Lewis: The Power of 'Good Trouble' | Timeless," The Library of Congress, July 19, 2020, https://blogs.loc.gov/loc/2020/07/remembering-john-lewis-the-power-of-good-trouble/.

5 Brian Tracy, *Change Your Thinking, Change Your Life: How to Unlock Your Full Potential for Success and Achievement* (Wiley, 2013), 107.

6 Joyce Meyer, *Do It Afraid: Embracing Courage in the Face of Fear*. First edition. (FaithWords, 2020).

7 Arch Wilkinson Shaw. *The Magazine of Business*, Vol. 52 (1927), 182.

8 Stuart Chen-Hayes, Melissa S. Ockerman, and E. C. M. Mason, *101 Solutions for School Counselors and Leaders in Challenging Times* (Corwin, 2014), 6.

9 Simon Sinek, *Start with Why: How Great Leaders Inspire Everyone to Take Action* (Portfolio/Penguin, 2009), 39.

10 "First-Generation Students in Higher Education – PNPI," n.d., https://pnpi.org/factsheets/first-generation-students/.

11 "School Connectedness Helps Students Thrive," Reducing Health Risks Among Youth, November 18, 2024, https://www.cdc.gov/youth-behavior/school-connectedness/index.html.

12 American School Counselor Association. *ASCA® National Model: A Framework for School Counseling Programs*. Fourth edition. (American School Counselor Association, 2019).

13 American School Counselor Association. *ASCA® National Model*.

14 Bradley Erford, (2011) *Transforming the School Counseling Profession*. 5th edition. (Pearson, 2011), v.

15 Qtd in. Tracy, *Change Your Thinking*, 69.

16 *ASCA® National Model*, 63.

17 Pamela J. Vaccaro, "The 80/20 Rule of Time Management," AAFP, September 15, 2000, https://www.aafp.org/pubs/fpm/issues/2000/0900/p76.html.

18 James Clear, *Atomic Habits: An Easy Way to Build Good Habits & Break Bad Ones* (Penguin Random House, 2018), 6.

19 Tracy, *Change Your Thinking*, 68.

20 Tracy, *Change Your Thinking*, 71.

21 G. Lynne Snead and Joyce Wycoff, *To Do...Doing...Done: A Creative Approach to Managing Projects and Effectively Finishing What Matters Most* (Simon & Schuster, 1997), 96.

22 The Fuller Center for Housing, "Famous Quotes by Millard Fuller - the Fuller Center for Housing," January 2, 2020, https://fullercenter.org/quotes/.

23 C.S. Lewis, introduction to On the Incarnation by Athanasius of Alexandria, trans. Penelope Lawson. (Sea Harp Press, 2022), 13.

24 Allison Edwards, *15-Minute Counseling Techniques that Work: What You Didn't Learn in Grad School* (National Center for Youth Issues, 2001), 4.

25, 27 Jim Collins, *Good to Great: Why Some Companies Make the Leap from Good to Great...and Others Don't*. (HarperCollins, 2001), 33-5, Window/Mirror Concept.

26 Collins, *Good to Great*, 90-119, Hedgehog Concept.

28 Karen Kaiser Clark, *Life Is Change: Growth Is Optional* (CEP Publications, 1993).

29 Mort Laitner, "'The Risk Taker'—A Mort Laitner Short Story | Mort Laitner," n.d., https://mortlaitner.com/what-do-you-mean-by-that-a-mort-laitner-short-story/#:~:text=%E2%80%9CHere's%20why%20I%20take%20risks,was%20sutured%20to%20their%20lips.

30 Clear, *Atomic Habits*, 93.

31 Clear, *Atomic Habits*, 84.

32 James Clear, "3-2-1: Failure, Mindset, and Relationships - James Clear," October 17, 2022. https://jamesclear.com/3-2-1/september-2-2021?rh_ref=6375c76f.

33 Les Brown, *The Ghosts of Who You Could Have Been*, Tiktok video, January 29, 2025, https://www.tiktok.com/tag/lesbrown.

34 David Wagoner, *Lost*, The Best American Poetry 2025, September 23, 2009, https://blog.bestamericanpoetry.com/the_best_american_poetry/2009/09/lost-by-david-wagoner.html

35 Robert Greenleaf, *Servant Leadership: A Journey into the Nature of Legitimate Power and Greatness* (Paulist Press, 2002), 27.

36 Plato, *Charmides, or Temperance*, trans. Benjamin Jowett, The Internet Classics Archive, n.d., https://classics.mit.edu/Plato/charmides.html.

37 Tracy, *Change Your Thinking*, 20.

38 Tracy, *Change Your Thinking*, 243.

39 David Belton and Bjorn Johnson, *Memory Box: Echoes of 9/11*. Documentary. MSNBC Films. 2021.

Permission to use ASCA® forms provided by Director of Communications, November 2024.

ABOUT THE AUTHORS

Dr. Sylvia A. Lopez is the former Director of Counseling Services for the second-largest school district in Texas. She spent forty-one years of her educational experience as a school counselor and as a principal in an elementary school, a middle school, and a high school. She also served as the Director of Counseling Services, where she facilitated the implementation of the school counseling program, coordinated district-wide initiatives, and actively supported and sponsored many of the College and Career Readiness Initiatives. In August 2017, Dr. Lopez retired to focus her work in other areas. Dr. Lopez co-founded the Lone Star State School Counselor Association (LSSSCA) in 2017. This association was formed to address the needs of school counselors and provide quality training and information for all school counselors across Texas. She also serves as a business consultant to help school district leaders understand the importance of a quality school counseling program by providing training and designing systems to benefit the school counselor. You may contact her at sylvialopez2006@gmail.com.

Dr. Tracey Brown served in the field of education for more than thirty years. She served as a teacher, school counselor, school counselor supervisor, mental health clinician, Director of Guidance, Counseling, and College Readiness, and Executive Director of Mental Health Services. In 2024, Dr. Brown retired from education to devote her life to ensure school counselors and mental health professionals have the tools they need to serve students with care and excellence. She continues to serve on various boards and design programs to enhance the mental health and counseling professions. Dr. Brown is the author of two books, *Single Mom, PhD* and *Ebb and Flow: A 21-Day Meditational Guide to Help You Recover from a Broken Heart and Broken Relationships*. She is a licensed professional counselor supervisor who works in private practice as a psychotherapist and mental health consultant. Visit her at: drtraceybrown.com

NATIONAL CENTER for
YOUTH ISSUES

About NCYI

National Center for Youth Issues provides educational resources, training, and support programs to foster the healthy social, emotional, and physical development of children and youth. Since our founding in 1981, NCYI has established a reputation as one of the country's leading providers of teaching materials and training for counseling and student-support professionals. NCYI helps meet the immediate needs of students throughout the nation by ensuring those who mentor them are well prepared to respond across the developmental spectrum.

Connect With Us Online!

@nationalcenterforyouthissues

@ncyi

@nationalcenterforyouthissues